THE INTERNET ECONOMY

THE INTERNET ECONOMY

ACCESS, TAXES, AND MARKET STRUCTURE

Alan E. Wiseman

BROOKINGS INSTITUTION PRESS
Washington, D.C.

33.8.47004678
W81 i

Copyright © 2000 by Alan E. Wiseman
Published by Brookings Institution Press
1775 Massachusetts Avenue, N.W., Washington, D.C. 20036
www.brookings.edu

Library of Congress Cataloging-in-Publication data
Wiseman, Alan E.
The Internet economy : access, taxes, and market structure / Alan E.
  Wiseman.
    p. cm.
Includes bibliographical references and index.
  ISBN 0-8157-9384-7 (acid-free paper)
1. Electronic commerce. 2. Electronic commerce—Taxation.
3. Internet—Economic aspects. I. Title.
HF5548.32 .W57 2000   00-010112
338.4'7004678—dc21   CIP

9 8 7 6 5 4 3 2 1

The paper used in this publication meets minimum requirements of the
American National Standard for Information Sciences—Permanence of
Paper for Printed Library Materials: ANSI Z39.48-1992.

Typeset in New Baskerville

Composition by Cynthia Stock
Silver Spring, Maryland

Printed by R. R. Donnelley and Sons
Harrisonburg, Virginia

CONTENTS

PREFACE

THIS BOOK IS the culmination of a project that arose in somewhat unusual circumstances and would never have been written without the help, support, and encouragement of a number of people. In early 1999, the middle of the third year of my doctoral program in political economics, a unique opportunity arose for me to take a position at the Federal Trade Commission, where I would split my time between serving as an economic research analyst at the Bureau of Economics and acting as an economic adviser to Commissioner Orson Swindle. With the encouragement of my faculty, I took a leave of absence from the Stanford University Graduate School of Business and jumped into my car the weekend after spring quarter finals ended. Driving across the country and arriving four days later in Washington, D.C., I reported for work on Monday, excited to begin.

Because I was only going to be in the commission for six months and I had expressed an interest in the Internet, I was given a very straightforward task: to learn about the Internet and electronic commerce, and to provide the bureau with a review of the relevant economic literature that could eventually be used as a reference guide. I remember thinking to myself: "O.K., I should have that done within a couple of weeks." How wrong I was.

I suddenly found myself immersed in a fascinating and rapidly expanding field of research, loosely classified as "Internet economics," that raised numerous compelling questions about how the Internet might change our economy. And for every answer that I hit upon, ten new issues arose that demanded attention. The Economic Issues Report that emerged from my efforts served as the foundation for this book.

This work will, I hope, serve several purposes. For scholars interested in the Internet economy, it indicates which questions have been asked and answered and what needs to be done next. For students of business, government, and economics, it provides some fundamental concepts regarding the Internet and economics and explains what information existing research can, and cannot, convey about the changes going on in the economy. And for the casual reader, it offers a new perspective on what is happening in today's quickly changing world.

That being said, several people deserve thanks for helping me bring this project to fruition. I am very grateful to Jeremy Bulow, the current director of the Bureau of Economics, who encouraged me to spend some time in Washington to learn about the Internet and antitrust policy. During my time there, the Federal Trade Commission and the Bureau of Economics, in particular, provided me with outstanding resources with which to conduct my research. Special thanks go to Daniel Caprio and Commissioner Orson Swindle for persuading me to take time away from Stanford to witness public policy from the driver's seat, and for giving me every opportunity to see how things worked once I arrived in Washington.

Along the way toward the final draft, I received very helpful comments from David Balto, Gerard Butters, Robert Cannon, Patrick DeGraba, Susan DeSanti, Michael Kende, David McAdams, Roger Noll, Thomas Pahl, Paul Pautler, Robert Pepper, Simon Steel,

Michael Vita, and Dean Williamson. Morgan Long and Melissa Oshfelt provided me with excellent research assistance, and Denis Breen read and offered outstanding criticisms and useful suggestions on virtually every draft of the work. In addition, Sara Harkavy enthusiastically helped me in many (sometimes tedious) phases of the writing.

At the Brookings Institution, I thank Robert Litan and Chris Kelaher for very helpful comments on earlier drafts and for encouraging me to pursue this project into its current form. Also thanks to Vicky Macintyre, who so ably edited my work, as well as Robert Elwood, who provided an index, and Carlotta Ribar, who proofread the pages. At Stanford University, I thank my faculty, David Baron and Keith Krehbiel in particular, for being outstanding teachers and for supporting me throughout my efforts as I "soaked and poked" in Washington. David and Jennifer Wiseman and Michael Steinberg provided me with much-welcomed encouragement and advice throughout the project, and in Washington, Elizabeth Chenoweth and Joy Ditto offered me their valuable friendship (and a great place to stay). I am also extremely appreciative of the constant support of Laura Veldkamp, who has been an inspiration in this and all endeavors.

Finally, I thank my parents, Israel and Trudy Wiseman, who have had unfaltering faith in me and over the years have driven me to press ahead. It is to them that I dedicate this book.

THE INTERNET ECONOMY

CHAPTER ONE

INTRODUCTION

THE TWENTIETH CENTURY has come to a close in the midst of a technological revolution that is affecting virtually every aspect of life in the
United States. An important part of this revolution is the expansion
of the Internet, which has triggered explosive growth in information technology. According to a 1999 study by the University of Texas
at Austin and Cisco Systems, the Internet economy, broadly defined
as those industries and professions that deal either directly or indirectly with the Internet, has already created more than 1.2 million
jobs and generated more $300 billion in revenue.[1] In terms of user
base, 72 million Americans are expected to have access to the web
by the end of 2000, up from 14.3 million in 1995.[2] The Internet, by
all accounts, has drastically changed the manner in which business
is done. Anything from material goods, such as groceries and compact discs, to information goods, such as database access and newspaper text, can be acquired with a mouse click or a keystroke.

The ease with which goods and services are purchased today is
the result of a dramatic rise of web-based businesses, known generally as electronic commerce, or "e-commerce." As of December 1999,

1. Barua and others (1999).
2. Atkinson and Court (1998).

1

there were more than 4.9 million commercial websites on the web, and that number was growing at a rate of almost 500,000 per month.[3] With the proliferation of commercial websites, not to mention the potential profits associated with such ventures, entrepreneurs have rushed in to carve out niches in this new marketplace. New market opportunities and business strategies that would have seemed fantastic years ago are quickly becoming commonplace.

New Practices and Problems

New business models are emerging everywhere. Recognizing the Internet's capacity for collecting valuable consumer information, firms have started giving away their products and services in exchange for data on consumers' tastes and preferences. In 1999 "Free-PC.com," for instance, presented computers to consumers who would allow themselves to be monitored online and targeted for advertisements.[4] Believing that the Internet could significantly streamline sales processes, IBM announced in October 1999 that it would be selling all of its desktop computers only on the web.[5] Even major consumer durables such as automobiles have found a place on the web: numerous sites now provide the 40 percent of potential customers who use the Internet in their car hunts with information to help them find their perfect rides.[6]

With these wondrous changes and the lowering of commercial barriers have come new debates and serious policy considerations

3. The term "commercial" website refers specifically to those websites that have a ".com" suffix. If one includes those commercial sites that use ".org," ".net," or some other suffix, then the number would be substantially larger. Estimates from: www.netcraft.com/survey/reports.

4. Hansell (1999a).

5. Hansell (1999b).

6. Swoboda and Brown (1999).

about what this technology will mean for international trade, education, and consumer welfare. One such question arose in November 1999, when the online bookstore Amazon.com began receiving orders for Adolf Hitler's *Mein Kampf* from buyers in Germany, where the German-language version is banned.[7] Another growing concern is the ease with which school children can download pornography and other inappropriate material from the Internet and whether schools and public libraries should install Internet filter software that would block access to such sites. These issues, in turn, have raised a host of questions about freedom of speech. Though investors and market analysts seem intrigued by these new market developments, not everyone is thrilled, as is evident from the 18,600 Internet-related complaints that the Federal Trade Commission received in 1999, up from 8,000 in 1998.[8] This statistic provides a mere glimmer of the growing attention that the legislative, executive, and regulatory arms of government are focusing on this new medium as they seek to understand it and its potential for both growth and misuse.

Learning about the "Information Economy"

What, precisely, is the "information economy," and how will the Internet affect our lives? In the United States, educational institutions have responded to this question with aggressive investigation. The Stanford Graduate School of Business, for one, has established the Center for Electronic Business and Commerce in the heart of Silicon Valley to study how the Internet and electronic commerce is affecting American society. Analogous research centers have been

7. Burgess (1999).
8. Drezen (2000).

established at numerous schools, including the Owen School of Management at Vanderbilt University, the Sloan School of Management at the Massachusetts Institute of Technology (MIT), and the University of Texas at Austin. The courses offered by professional schools across the country run the gamut from "Internet and Society: Technologies and Politics of Control" (Harvard Law School) to "Internet Ventures" (University of Chicago Law School) and "Internet Strategy and Marketing" (Yale School of Management). It is hard to imagine that ten years ago any of these topics would have been considered appropriate for professional school training, yet today many are viewed as necessary components of any curriculum.

Amid the great acclaim that media commentators heap on the Internet, some wonder how much of this is "hype" and to what extent the "digital revolution" can really affect the world. Now that a variety of new business models are taking hold, it seems timely to ask how the government might become involved in Internet-related issues. So far, government entities seem to have been hesitant to intervene for fear of throwing a proverbial monkey wrench into the works of (what appears to be) an exceptionally smooth economy. According to a recent report by the International Competition Policy Advisory Committee, for example, the expansion of e-commerce could pose several threats to competition, notably through cartel creation and price signaling. While not offering any specific policy recommendations, the committee urged governments to be very attentive to the ongoing development of the e-marketplace, and to be ready to respond with appropriate antitrust enforcement measures.[9]

The government's reluctance to take action without further guidance raises some important questions for economic practitioners and politicians. A fundamental question is whether new theories

9. ICPAC (2000).

need to be constructed in order to explain the internal workings of the digital market? Or do "a few basic economic concepts go a long way toward explaining how today's industries are evolving"?[10] I try to answer this question in the pages that follow.

One important task in such an exercise is to review some of the recent literature dealing with the economics of the Internet, especially in relation to the pricing of access to the Internet, the pricing of goods sold via the Internet, network externalities, and Internet taxation. This makes it possible to collect some thoughts about the future development of the Internet with respect to market structure, consumer welfare, and likely areas of government intervention. While none of these topics is covered in complete detail, this book provides a roadmap of the current terrain in Internet-related economic matters, as well as a framework for future analysis.[11]

The discussion begins in chapter 2 with a brief nontechnical description of the origins and current state of the Internet and an outline of the technologies discussed in subsequent chapters. Chapter 3 covers current pricing practices for providing Internet access, as well as theoretical possibilities that have yet to be implemented. Chapter 4 takes up the question of how the environment of the Internet, especially with respect to its relatively low search costs and a variety of easy-access information, will shape the pricing of goods and services sold online. The literature pertaining to network externalities is the subject of chapter 5, which also touches on the

10. Shapiro and Varian (1999: 2).

11. The topics covered in this book were selected for investigation primarily because of the sizable body of existing (and relevant) economic research. A nonexhaustive list of additional Internet-related topics might include commercial fraud, electronic payment systems, security and privacy of Internet transactions, copyright protection, and advertising strategies. For a discussion of several of these subjects, see Choi, Stahl, and Whinston (1997); Litan (1999); Shapiro and Varian (1999); and Swire and Litan (1998).

possible application of theoretical models of network creation to the current state of the Internet. Chapter 6 moves beyond theoretical and empirical studies to a topic of widespread interest at present: taxation of online commerce. Chapter 7 brings the discussion to a close with some general observations and comments about possible areas of future research.

The phrase "we are living in interesting times" seems more applicable now than at any other time in history. The Internet could well enable us to realize some of our grandest science-fiction-based visions of the future. Many of us have dreamed of conducting all of our necessary transactions and communications electronically, earning our bachelor's or advanced degrees from our living room, and accessing all forms of recorded or processed information on demand. While such activities seem feasible and by some measures attractive, a great deal of uncertainty remains as to how these fast-emerging markets will stabilize, who the dominant players will be in tomorrow's economy, and how government activity might help or hinder those who seek to harness the full potential of the Internet. This book is a first step toward understanding what economics can tell us about where we are going and where we need to look next.

CHAPTER TWO

WHAT IS
THE INTERNET?

THIS CHAPTER PRESENTS a brief sketch of the technological development of the Internet.[1] The transmission technologies described here
(packet switching versus circuit switching) play an important role in
models of access pricing.

The technology currently referred to as the Internet originated
in the early 1960s when a division of the Department of Defense,
the Advanced Research Projects Administration (ARPA), developed
a system called the ARPAnet to link together universities and high-
tech defense contractors. ARPAnet was actually a by-product of the
search for a communications network that could link branches of
government likely to escape destruction in the event of war. The

---

1. In this book the term "Internet" refers to an open network. The Federal
Networking Council (FNC) defines the Internet as "the global information system that—(i) is logically linked together by a globally unique address space
based on the Internet Protocol (IP) or its subsequent extensions/follow-ons;
(ii) is able to support communications using the Transmission Control Proto-
col/Internet Protocol (TCP/IP) suite or its subsequent extensions/follow-ons,
and/or other IP-compatible protocols; and (iii) provides, uses or makes accessible, either publicly of privately, high level services layered on the communications and related infrastructure described herein." (FNC Resolutions: Definition
of "Internet," 10/24/95, www.fnc.gov/Internet_res.html). In contrast, the web
is an application that runs on that network.

thinking was that information transmitted on (what we now call) the Internet—since it traveled via packets rather than closed circuits—would still get through even if certain telephone networks were destroyed because such packets would find whatever pathways were still available.[2]

In October 1969 a message was successfully transmitted between research centers at the University of California at Los Angeles and the Stanford Research Institute in Northern California, and the Internet was born. Government involvement in the evolution of the Internet continued into the 1980s when the National Science Foundation (NSF) created NSFNET to connect the NSF-funded supercomputer centers. The NSFNET evolved as a backbone network serving several smaller regional networks and their supported local area networks (LAN). About the same time, several private Internet backbones began to emerge, providing access to private networks in a manner analogous to NSFNET. By 1994 there were three such privately funded networks in the United States besides NSFNET: Alternet, PSInet, and SprintLink. With the success of these ventures, the federal government withdrew from backbone provision in 1995, when NSF funding for NSFNET expired. However, the NSF helped coordinate the development of interconnection points between backbones, known as Network Access Points (NAPs), which are currently operated by private entities.[3]

2. Tapscott (1996: 17–19).

3. For more detailed information on the history and technology of the Internet, see Abbate (1999); Esbin (1998); Krol and Klopfenstein (1996); MacKie-Mason and Varian (1997); and Oxman (1999). Galla (1998) provides a nontechnical introduction and explanation of recent Internet technologies, and Greenstein (1999) provides a history of the Internet Service Provider market. See also the Internet Society's webpage, "Internet Histories," at www.isoc.org/internet/history/index.shtml.

Basic Technology and Infrastructure

Because it has no central authority and consists of several components connected by an open communications standard, the Internet is commonly referred to as a "network of networks." This is not to say that no organizations exist to oversee Internet development; as explained shortly, numerous groups have emerged to act in this capacity. The infrastructure is organized in a straightforward hierarchy consisting of backbone providers at the top, regional networks next, and LAN at the bottom.[4] A backbone can be thought of as an interstate highway, stretching from one side of the nation to the other and connecting to smaller intrastate highways. These smaller intrastate pathways are like regional networks that connect individual city roads to the interstate highway. The LAN, such as those on a university campus, are like city and country roads connecting smaller points.

The Internet also resembles a road system in the manner in which information is transmitted. As already mentioned, the Internet does not employ circuit-switching technology, as telephone networks do, but utilizes a packet-switching technology. In the case of "circuit switching," a circuit must be established between two customers before they can make a phone call, and that circuit must remain open for the entire duration of the call, even in periods of dead silence. In highway terms, circuit switching would be analogous to closing off an entire lane of the interstate for a person who wanted to send a dozen roses from San Francisco to Washington, D.C., and that lane would remain closed until the flowers were delivered.[5] The

---

4. For more information on this three-tier structure, see MacKie-Mason and Varian (1997).

5. This illustration disregards teleflorists, of course.

Internet, by contrast, allows more than one sender to transmit data along a pathway at the same time. The data travel in small "packets," usually consisting of approximately 200 bytes, which do not require a dedicated circuit. To return to the highway analogy, packet switching is comparable to transporting each of the dozen roses in a separate car, and then reassembling the entire package once they all reach their destination. The time of delivery, of course, would depend upon the quality of the road, and on the amount of traffic encountered in transit.

Two other distinctive features of the Internet have to do with how the information is broken down into packets and how the packets are reassembled. The technology that allows such data transmission to occur is known as the TCP/IP protocol. When a user at a given terminal sends data such as an e-mail message or a webpage on the Internet "highway," the message is first broken down into packets by the transmission control protocol (TCP), which also attaches a "header" to each packet specifying how all are to be recombined at their destination. Once the packets are created, the internet protocol (IP) provides each packet with address information directing it to the next stop on its journey between points.

All e-mail addresses and webpages have a unique IP address consisting of four numbers, each ranging from 0 to 255 and separated by periods (dots). This represents the "mailing address" of the computer to which the content is being sent. Conventional e-mail addresses and webpage names (for example, student@stanford.edu, www.gsb.stanford.edu) are used only as a mnemonic device. Upon sending e-mail, or requesting a webpage, a name server translates the e-mail address or webpage name into its corresponding IP address to determine where precisely the message is going on the Internet. For example, the IP address for the home page of Stanford University (www.stanford.edu) is 171.64.14.237.

Between their point of origin and final destination, packets may cross several computer networks analogous to interstate (backbone) and intrastate (regional network) highways. At each junction between networks, a "router" examines the packet and its IP address and then determines where to send it next in order to manage traffic most efficiently. When the packets reach their final destination, the TCP reassembles them into their original form.

Although the process seems simple enough, congestion on the network during periods of high user activity can severely inhibit delivery time and performance. As yet most networks have no means of addressing the traffic problem and do not assign priority classes for packets. Delivery remains almost instantaneous when traffic is low, but during high traffic packets enter a queue and are usually transmitted on a first-in-first-out (FIFO) basis, regardless of their importance. As a result, some packets may be substantially delayed or discarded altogether. In the case of dropped packets, further delay can ensue as the TCP, in recognizing packet loss as a symptom of high traffic, may reduce the rate at which packets are sent as it attempts to relieve congestion.

New technologies are helping to ameliorate this congestion without having to ration access. "Broadband" Internet services, for example—through either cable, satellite, or conventional copper telephone lines (through DSL)—are enabling consumers to surf the web at much higher speeds. As the Internet becomes increasingly popular, of course, congestion may arise with these technologies too, absent any sort of rationing mechanism.[6]

---

6. For a broad overview of these topics, see Kopel (1999) and chapter 3 in this volume.

Governance Structure

As just mentioned, at this time no centralized authority governs the Internet. While the infrastructure is continuously being developed through a combination of public and private investment, different parts of the network operate more or less independently. Industry consortiums and volunteer nonprofit groups such as the World Wide Web Consortium (W3C), the Internet Engineering Task Force (IETF), and the Internet Corporation for Assigned Names and Numbers (ICANN) have emerged in recent years to help devise universal standards for interoperability, but none of these bodies possess any sort of de facto law-making power with which to establish general rules of web "etiquette." A matter of wide interest being dealt with by one of these consortiums is domain names registration. A domain name is the term given to the proper name assigned to the IP address of a webpage (for example, www.washington post.com).

Network Solutions Incorporated (NSI) of Herndon, Virginia, currently maintains the domain name registry. Under the terms of a contract awarded in 1992 by the Department of Commerce and extending to 1998, NSI held a virtual monopoly over registering websites ending in several suffixes (including .com, .edu, and .net). Anticipating the contract's expiration, the Clinton administration charged ICANN with investigating ways of managing domain name registration more efficiently. An agreement hammered out between the Department of Commerce and NSI in September 1999 paved the way for open competition in domain name registration: NSI agreed to make a one-time grant of $1.25 million to ICANN to help cover its administrative fees and to formally recognize ICANN's administrative authority over domain name registration, while NSI retained control over the domain name database until 2003 (at which point a successor registry, possibly NSI, was to be designated).[7] The agreement facilitated competition by enabling other firms to handle domain name registration, providing that they paid NSI a fee of $6 to enter each new name in NSI's database.

The agreement did not specify the process by which ICANN would designate the new registrar, but it did provide NSI with financial incentives to withdraw from the registration business.[8] If the registry was sold to another company in the first eighteen months after the agreement was ratified (in November 1999), the purchaser of the registry was to have administrative authority over domain names for an additional four years after 2003 (thereby increasing the sale price, other things being equal).[9] In March 2000 NSI was purchased by VeriSign Inc., a producer of online security software, for $21 billion in VeriSign stock. Under the terms of the deal, NSI will still control the registry, but VeriSign will have access to the entire database, including its contact information.[10]

The issue of domain names aside, the explosive growth of the web in recent years combined with the lack of central authority has raised some serious questions about the appropriate role of government (federal or otherwise) in managing the web. Many in industry

7. For more information on the agreement, see www.icann.org/nsi/nsi-registry-agreement.htm.

8. Kaplan and Schriver (1999).

9. NSI also registers domain names itself, charging anywhere from $35 to $169, depending upon the registration options desired (length of registration, listing in a directory, and the like). In a response to a request for comment (RFC) by the National Telecommunications and Information Administration, Vita and Horne (1998) provide a technical overview of domain name assignment as well as the competitive implications of the breakup of NSI's monopoly over assignment power. For more information on the development of Internet governance and domain name assignment, see Gillet and Kapor (1997); Shaw (1997); Gigante (1997); and Oppendahl (1997).

10. Wheeler (2000).

believe that both electronic commerce and other Internet matters
should be regulated by the private sector.[11] Various advocacy groups,
however, have pressed for government involvement in policy issues
ranging from privacy to access provision to sales tax. Whatever role
the federal government adopts in the future, be it legislative or regulatory (under the auspices, say, of the Department of Justice, DOJ;
Federal Communications Commission, FCC; or the Federal Trade
Commission, FTC), the topics addressed in the following chapters
are likely to be among the more relevant issues at the forefront of
the policy debate.

---

11. For an explanation of how the private marketplace and minimal government intervention has allowed the Internet to thrive, see Oxman (1999).

CHAPTER THREE

PRICING
ACCESS

AN INTERESTING ASPECT of Internet activity is that user preferences regarding the number of other network users are somewhat mixed. As more consumers and businesses use the Internet, the value of the network to any given user increases. However, this positive trend continues only until congestion becomes so great that service deteriorates because of excessive delay or disappears altogether.[1] With the explosive growth in the number of web-users and the increased use of data-intensive applications (such as streaming audio and video), a major concern today is how best to manage Internet traffic in order to ensure high levels of service quality. Several technological innovations have been suggested to address potential congestion problems, and scholarly attention has also been concentrated on distribution, particularly on pricing mechanisms that can lead to efficient use of network resources.

Taken together, these pricing models draw on traditional microeconomic theory and more recent computer science. They range from simple methods, such as flat pricing for access, to more complicated approaches, such as conducting auctions over individual

1. Economists would argue that such preferences are indicative of the concavity of a user's utility function over network activity.

packets. This chapter examines several of these pricing approaches, some supply-side alternatives that might improve Internet traffic, and several public policy aspects of access provision.[2]

Flat Pricing

The most common method currently used to distribute access to the Internet is flat pricing. Users pay a flat fee, usually monthly, that allows them to have unlimited access to the Internet at a particular service level. For example, for $19.95 a month, a customer may be connected to an Internet service provider (ISP) and allowed unlimited use at whatever speed the modem pool of the ISP supports. Flat pricing essentially offers "best-effort" service for all users. When the network is uncongested, waiting time is negligible, and all information is transmitted instantaneously. When usage is high, however, flat pricing cannot discriminate between users, and all customers are subject to the same degree of delays and loss in service quality. This is not to imply that other pricing systems could necessarily provide a better transmission path or guaranteed delivery. Rather, by differentiating between packets, other pricing mechanisms might be able to provide users willing to pay higher prices with a higher quality of service than that available when all packets are treated alike.

In some applications (for example, e-mail), delayed transmission might have little effect, whereas in others (such as real-time video or audio streams) delayed or dropped packets could be a serious problem. That is one reason why the current lack of coordination on the Internet and its potential for creating numerous traffic

2. The approaches discussed here represent just a sample of the relevant microeconomic research concerned with Internet congestion. For additional examples and references, see McKnight and Bailey (1997).

bottlenecks is a growing concern.[3] Without a "centralized mechanism" to manage traffic during sporadic jams either on the backbone or at various switch points on the local exchange carrier (LEC), service is bound to suffer.

Despite these problems, proponents of flat pricing argue that it is more convenient for both consumers and providers in that it simplifies accounting, encourages use, and provides a guaranteed stream of revenue with which ISPs can recover the high sunk costs associated with developing network infrastructure.[4] Because it costs almost nothing to provide access to a user once the infrastructure is developed, charging the marginal cost of production of access (which is conventionally associated with the "efficient" competitive outcome) would make price necessarily equal to zero. Such a pricing schedule, though indicative of a competitive outcome, would make it impossible to recover the costs expended by developing the network, and hence to induce private parties to take on the significant investments that accompany network development.

Revenue and accounting issues aside, the conveniences of flat pricing have their inefficiencies, too. First, and most obvious, the flat price does not induce users to take into account the congestion costs (an externality) that they impose on other users during peak periods. Given that users are charged the same price to send data regardless of when the data are sent (essentially nothing, given that they have paid for access already), each user is faced with the classic prisoner's dilemma: individuals would be happier if others stayed off the network during periods of congestion, but each user would prefer to send a transmission and wait a bit, rather than get off the network altogether. As a result, as one would expect, users continue

3. See Werbach (1997).
4. Anania and Solomon (1997); Clark (1997).

to log onto the network, even in periods of high congestion, and cause service to deteriorate. A concrete example of this real-world tragedy-of-the-commons comes from the 1996 experience with pricing mechanisms at America Online (AOL).[5] When AOL switched from usage-sensitive pricing to flat pricing, users flooded the system, at times leaving their connections on unattended; this caused excessive delays and, at times, a complete system breakdown.

Another, closely related problem is that the flat price does not discriminate between "high" and "low" value applications. As a result, a teenager sending a video stream of his summer vacation can plausibly take precedence over a video conference call of a Fortune 500 company. Even if the company would be willing to pay a premium for higher-quality service, most current flat-pricing packages do not provide such an option. In view of the lack of discrimination and the poor quality of "high-priority" applications when traffic piles up on the network, more attention is being given to usage-sensitive and priority-sensitive pricing mechanisms that could, in theory, lead to a more efficient allocation of resources than could be accomplished by the flat-pricing scheme.

Auction Approach

One alternative pricing scheme proposed by Jeffrey MacKie-Mason and Hal Varian is a per-packet auction pricing that would vary with the level of congestion on the network.[6] Recall that most of the costs associated with backbone networks are fixed costs incurred during the building of infrastructure. In times when the network is not saturated, the cost (that is, delay time) of sending a message is

---

5. For details, see Odlyzko (1997).
6. See MacKie-Mason and Varian (1993, 1995, 1997).

zero, and packets travel seamlessly from sender to receiver. In times of high congestion, however, packets are delayed and dropped from the queue, and later re-sent from their point of origin.

Under the per-packet auction system, the incremental costs of sending a packet would be zero when the network is uncongested (to accurately reflect the social costs of the transaction at that time). The social costs of delaying the packets of other users would be internalized by a given user and be positive. And funding for the infrastructure would be covered by a fixed connection fee that would vary from one consumer to another as a function of their relative willingness to pay. Each user would pay a flat fee for connection to the network and then submit a "bid" with each packet for the amount that he or she would be willing to pay to have that packet transmitted. In this "smart market," the "bid" would be submitted by attaching it to the header of the packet and would only be a bid for the relative priority of service, in the sense that higher-bid packets would enter the queue before lower-bid packets. However, it would be impossible to guarantee priority in delivery because of network issues at the other end of the transaction.[7]

Given this specification, the price paid at each router by a given bidder would be the market-clearing price, defined as the bid submitted by the first person whose packet is not sent owing to the capacity constraints of the network and the range of bids submitted. On the Internet, then, if a router could forward only five packets, and ten packets were submitted for consideration with bids attached, then the first five highest-valued packets would be accepted and sent on, and the users whose packets were sent would pay the

---

7. The authors note that IP addresses currently contain fields for "priority" or "type of service" (TOS) specifications. Hence, using a subsection of the IP address as a bid field seems technologically feasible.

bid attached to the sixth highest-valued packet.[8] The use of an auction in this setting could boost efficiency in several respects. First,
the smart market would induce customers to pay nonzero positive
prices when the social costs of their packet transmissions are positive, while paying prices equal to zero when the network is
uncongested. Second, this mechanism would function like the well-
established mechanism known as the Vickrey auction, in which the
dominant strategy is to bid the bidder's true valuation of the item
being sold (in this case, packets).[9] Hence, from an efficiency standpoint, the smart market ensures that bidders will not misrepresent
their valuations and lead them to pay more, or less, than the true
valuation of their transmissions.[10] Third, the revenues generated

8. It should be evident that the sixth-highest bid is the marginal bid, because users who submitted a lesser bid would strictly prefer to keep their money
rather than pay the sixth-highest price for service. Conversely, users who submitted a bid greater than the sixth-highest bid would strictly prefer to pay the
sixth-highest bid over their own bid for packet transmission. Finally, individuals
who submitted the sixth-highest bid, if that was their true valuation for service,
should be indifferent about paying for their service and keeping their money
without transmission.

9. In a Vickrey auction (Vickrey 1961), bidding one's valuation is a dominant strategy because the value of a user's bid only affects the price that a user
pays when he is the marginal bidder. In such a situation, if a user were to over-
bid his true valuation, the only time it would change the outcome would be
when he received service but paid a price higher than his valuation. Conversely,
if a user underbid his true valuation, the only time it would change the outcome would be when he was denied service despite having a higher actual value
for the service than the posted price. Hence, a user can do no better than simply bidding his true valuation for the product in question.

10. MacKie-Mason and Varian's (1993, 1995, 1997) claims about truth-telling being a dominant strategy in their smart market are somewhat question-
able because their auction is more representative of a uniform-price auction
than a multi-unit Vickrey auction. Ausubel and Cramton (1998) explain that
the uniform-price auction does not possess the efficiency properties of the multi-
unit Vickrey auction, particularly with respect to truth-telling.

from such a mechanism will equal the optimal level of investment in infrastructure capacity.

One drawback of the proposed smart market, MacKie-Mason and Varian note, is that many individuals might not find the notion of fluctuating access prices attractive. Of course, such fluctuation will occur less often as prices and availability become more predictable through the use of the market. Furthermore, the smart market should experience only downward price fluctuations with respect to a bidder's expectations.[11] In addition, institutions such as intermediate sellers can emerge in this market to sell to end-users who are hesitant to enter the market directly.

While some have questioned whether MacKie-Mason and Varian's smart market can accommodate the inherent "burstiness" (quick fluctuations in traffic over short periods of time) of many packet transfers, the technology apparently exists to handle the complications that accompany such burstiness. Furthermore, the smart market, when implemented properly, should contribute to an overall decline in burstiness.[12]

Static Priority Pricing

A third model of access pricing proposed by Ron Cocchi and others provides for packets being assigned a priority position whenever placed in a queue because of network congestion.[13] The basic

11. Because a bidder is only paying the marginal price of service, any large "fluctuations" in price should occur as large downward shifts from the expected price paid, if the marginal user has a far lower valuation for the service than a given bidder.

12. See MacKie-Mason and Varian (1995) for details on ways to handle these plausible complications.

13. See Cocchi and others (1993). Variants are discussed in Braden, Clark, and Shenker (1994); Clark, Shenker, and Zhang (1992); Shenker (1995); and Shenker, Clark, and Zhang (1993).

assumption here is that users are likely to place different weights on the value of quick access to the network, depending upon what sort of application is being used. For example, it is reasonable to believe that most users would be willing to tolerate delays in e-mail packet delivery, but less willing to tolerate delays in real-time audio or video transmission. In view of this difference in delay valuation, this model establishes different priority classes for the network (as a function of expected delay) and allows users to select the priority class they would prefer for their packets. This means the network itself would not be partitioned into different priority classes; rather, "priorities" would be assigned to packets when they are sent and would represent their position in the queue should the network become congested (at which point, they would be handled according to FIFO).

A priority system must obviously attach some sort of pricing scheme to its different classes in order to induce efficient self-selection into the classes.[14] In the model just described, users' utilities are defined in terms of the value (negative) that they place on the delay time for a given packet and the amount of money that they pay for transmission. The sequence of events consists of users simply placing an order for service at a particular priority level, paying the fee associated with that priority level, and having their packets sent. When tested in a general framework, the model constructs feasible prices for different priority classes that maximize aggregate welfare for all users in the network. The prices for priority classes are not updated every period in response to the level of network traffic; rather, before making their service request, users must choose from an unchanging (static) menu of priority levels. Simulations in which users selected service levels for four different applications

14. Without monetary considerations, all users would have an incentive to specify the highest priority level for all of their applications, and the network would be just as congested as if there were no priority classes.

(e-mail, FTP, telnet, video) demonstrate that a static two-priority ("high" and "low") pricing system can generate the socially desirable congestion level for a wide array of network configurations and load usage.

Despite its attractive implementation properties, especially from an accounting standpoint, this pricing system raises some concerns for the network designer.[15] First, because the prices are unchanging with respect to network load, as a matter of efficiency, users may now and again pay inappropriate amounts for the level of service they request. When the network is completely uncongested, for example, high-priority users will be overpaying to have the same service as low-priority users (essentially, no delay), and conversely, when there is excessive congestion, high-priority users may be underpaying and hence may create further congestion. While it is true that these effects might "even out" in expectation, on a point-by-point basis, it seems that a more dynamic approach to network pricing may be more desirable.

Some have also questioned whether such a system can actually be implemented on a large network where a central planner might have limited information about users' priority preferences.[16] While that might make it more difficult to achieve efficient priority prices, implementing some sort of differential pricing scheme between priority levels, even in a static setting, appears likely to enhance social welfare.[17]

15. When trying to assess charges, there is no need to worry about what path a given packet takes. Users are assessed a simple entry fee per application for a given priority level, and then the system does the best it can to provide service.

16. Gupta, Stahl, and Whinston (1997a).

17. Citing the postal system's mailing policies (for example, overnight, priority mail, standard first class), Einhorn (1995) also speaks of the virtues of static-priority pricing schemes as a technologically feasible and welfare-enhancing pricing mechanism.

Dynamic Priority Pricing

A more complicated model of priority pricing has also been developed to enhance Internet efficiency.[18] A basic premise of this approach, proposed by Alok Gupta and others, is that the efficiency properties associated with the auction approach are contingent on two conditions: all potential packets must be present at the auction, and the value of a packet is independent of the conditional passage of other packets. Both of these conditions are likely violated in the Internet environment because delays can always be expected at congestion points between packet arrival and bids, and the value of packets is affected by the drop rates in the network.

To address these problems, a dynamic priority-pricing scheme should be devised that is anchored in a theoretical base (such as microeconomic theory). Furthermore, it must be operational and adjust prices in real time. The overhead costs associated with implementing such a system should be manageable, and the model should be adequately tested before being deployed onto a network. These conditions, it is theorized, could be met through a priority-pricing mechanism implemented in a completely decentralized environment; and through simulation, it could be shown to be more efficient than a flat-pricing model for network access.

Consider now a general equilibrium framework that generically incorporates the preferences of all relevant users and service providers; in addition, suppose that users are faced with access options varying in estimated delay times, price, and quality of service and choose the expected optimal access option.[19] In such circumstances, one can expect a "stochastic equilibrium" that has the following

18. See Gupta, Stahl, and Winston (1995, 1996, 1997b, 1997c).
19. Economists would refer to this choice as choosing to maximize one's "ex ante utility."

properties: "average flow rates of service are optimal for each user given the prices and anticipated delay, and . . . the anticipated delays are correct ex-ante expected delays given the average flow rates."[20] The adoption of stochastic equilibrium prices will, in turn, maximize social welfare.

This model operates in countable periods (discrete time), and in each period a user is presented with a menu of options listing the relative prices for different priority classes as a function of delay time or other qualities. After considering each option, a user (or perhaps an electronic agent that has been programmed with the user's preferences) selects the preferred option (which might include not using any service at all, as would manifest itself in best-effort service). Once the option is selected, it is sent to the least-cost available server, where it is immediately processed if the queue is empty. If other jobs are waiting in the queue, users' requests are processed on a FIFO basis, depending on their priority class. The estimates for prices in the user's initial menu are updated every T units of time, and the actual prices in period $(t + 1)$ are a function of the prices in period (t) and expected prices in period $(t + 1)$ (where prices are positively correlated with delay times in the previous period, which increases with the number of users on the system).[21]

Updating takes place every T period rather than when service requests are made for three reasons. First, estimating delays and prices over longer periods of time produces more stable results. Second, small perturbations in prices will not warrant frequent updates once a stochastic equilibrium is realized. Third (this is the most compelling argument, given that this model is meant to be

20. This latter condition intuitively means that on the condition that the average level of user traffic is known, users' expectations about plausible delay times will be realized. See Gupta and others (1995: 5).

21. Formally, they assume that price in period $(t + 1) = \alpha \times$ (expected price in period $(t + 1)) + (1 - \alpha) \times$ (price in period (t)), where $\alpha \in (0, 1)$.

practical), the computational effort associated with updating following each service request is likely to be prohibitively high.

In simulations that employ perfect and imperfect information regarding delay times and that compare aggregate welfare under systems of free access to the network, flat pricing, and priority pricing, a dynamic priority-pricing system does better than both free access and flat pricing. These results are not so surprising in cases of perfect information about delay times. Even when prices are a function of expected delay, however, the priority-pricing model generates higher social welfare than the other two options because the imposition of prices for different service levels effectively constrains congestion.

An especially attractive feature of both the static and the stochastic equilibrium model is that accounting is very manageable. All entities in the transmission chain are presented with only one bill, which represents the cost of sending a packet to the next node in the network. Of course, in equilibrium, subsequent transmission costs between links are accounted for in the bill presented to the prior link. Thus far, however, no simulations have been attempted to compare the dynamic priority-pricing model with the auction approach under particular assumptions about user demands for timeliness, price, and other parameters. Nevertheless, dynamic priority pricing seems to be a practical and desirable alternative to current flat-pricing practices.[22]

PMP Approach

Yet another approach in which users sort themselves according to their respective budget constraints is known as the Paris Metro pric-

---

22. This conclusion rests, of course, on the availability of relevant supporting technologies.

ing (PMP) approach.[23] In this model, developed by Andrew Odlyzko, the network is partitioned into independent routes and different prices are assigned to access to each route. The model is named after the Paris train system, which, until the 1980s, contained first- and second-class seats identical in number and quality, but priced differently (first-class seats cost more). This difference in price led to a de facto difference in quality between the first- and second-class cars: more people purchased second-class tickets and congestion on second-class cars increased, while first-class cars remained less occupied and hence more comfortable.

When this intuition is applied to the Internet environment, the different prices assigned to the routes will not reflect differences in precedence levels across routes or different quality-of-service guarantees, as in the static priority-pricing model. Rather, the differences in transmission costs will lead to expected differences in quality of service on the part of users, as in the Paris Metro system. These expected differences will be realized as users sort themselves according to their willingness to pay, and hence congestion levels decline (service improves) on the higher-priced channels. One attractive property of the PMP system is that once developed, it is relatively inexpensive to administer. From a technical standpoint, it should also be easy to implement, given that current Internet protocol standards could be altered to designate what paths of the network a given packet may take.[24]

Although in principle the PMP seems simple to deploy, it has two main practical problems that can affect efficiency. First, for applica-

23. See Odlyzko (1997, 1999a, 1999b).

24. As of 1997, when the theory was developed, IPv4 packets had a three-bit priority field that was unused (Odlyzko 1997: 9). In theory, it would be simple to assign a network class to this priority field that would designate which portion of the network the packet would use for transmission.

tions to run well, traffic on the system must be on the low side, which raises questions about how to partition the network to ensure that portions of it are not being under- or overutilized. Second, from a technical standpoint, current technologies (as of 1999) make it extremely difficult to actually measure the traffic on the Internet, and thus to design efficient partitions. These technical concerns aside, the PMP system seems attractive in the sense that high-priority applications would not experience the numerous delays common under a flat-pricing mechanism.

Expected Capacity Pricing

Yet another scheme that might ameliorate the efficiency concerns surrounding flat pricing is the "expected capacity pricing" mechanism proposed by David Clark.[25] In this case, all users send their packets on the same network, but before transmission they make contracts with network access points and pay for the amount of excess capacity to be provided. Such contracts can be considered a form of insurance for priority treatment in the case of congestion. Whenever the network is uncongested, all packets are treated identically and forwarded between routers. In the event of high traffic and congestion, the excess capacity contracts take effect. Those packets that have contracted for sufficient excess capacity are forwarded, whereas those that have not must wait in the queue, with their position depending on how much capacity they have reserved.

Although such a pricing policy would not necessarily affect the overall level of network congestion, like the static priority-pricing scheme, it should enhance efficiency by sorting high- and low-priority users by their willingness to pay. By providing "priority in-

25. See Clark (1997).

surance" for those entering the queue, the scheme should ensure that network resources are devoted to those who value them most at any given point in time.

Summary and Implications

According to one estimate, the number of U.S. households connected to the Internet is expected to reach almost 60 million in 2003, compared with only 33 million in 1998.[26] Estimates that take into account the number of adults connected to the Internet at the end of the century are even higher, ranging from 72 million to 110 million.[27] Another estimate places the number of web users in 2001 at 175 million.[28]

This growth in web usage is expected to be matched by more data-intensive real-time applications such as Internet telephony and video conferencing. These two trends will likely lead to a substantial increase in demand, not only for access more generally but also for high-speed access, particularly that provided by broadband technologies (DSL, cable modem). Once underexposed populations in other continents gain access, standard service under a flat-pricing regime may deteriorate significantly unless steps are taken to manage congestion, whether through pricing policies or technological innovation.

On the supply side, recent technological developments might serve to ameliorate congestion, absent changes in pricing. Even a simple increase in backbone capacity can help to solve congestion-related problems,[29] although some observers argue that such ex-

26. Carmel, Eisenach, and Lenard (1999).
27. Carmel and others (1999); www.c-i-a.com/199911iu.htm.
28. Thompson (2000).
29. Werbach (1997).

pansion would actually increase congestion because users, assuming that the Internet can handle even more data-intensive applications and provide higher levels of service, would step up web usage more than they ever would otherwise.[30] Consider what happens when a city expands a highway system from two to three lanes. Does this effectively constrain traffic? Not likely. If anything, more travelers choose to use the highway, believing that the increase in capacity will reduce their travel time. This increase in usage, Bernardo Huberman claims, would likely cancel out the efficiency that might normally be gained through capacity expansion.

Another technological alternative is to employ "caching" technologies. They reduce Internet traffic by aggregating and maintaining content (such as an electronic newspaper's webpage) in a location that is easily accessible to a pool of users, rather than requiring these users to individually seek the content at its original source.[31] Various technological protocols are also available to differentiate levels of service, and when combined with an appropriate pricing scheme, they can help alleviate congestion.[32]

Although these supply-side alternatives might prove useful in reducing congestion, experiences in Berkeley, California, and New Zealand have shown that various usage-sensitive pricing mechanisms can have a more significant impact on consumers' Internet usage patterns.[33] Such mechanisms have long been advocated as an effi-

30. Huberman (1997).
31. Some have asked whether caching can cause other difficulties, in that the content being stored on the local server can easily become out of date or obsolete between the time that it is originally downloaded and it is finally viewed by a user. Proponents of caching argue that such problems will eventually be solved through technological innovations. See Thompson (1999, 2000).
32. See Werbach (1997); Mace (2000).
33. On Berkeley, see Edell, McKeown, and Varaiaya (1994); on New Zealand, Brownlee (1996).

cient way to manage road (network) resources to avoid automobile congestion.[34] Hence, from a theoretical standpoint, it seems that some of the options discussed in this chapter could solve congestion problems under certain conditions and might even provide an "efficient" allocation of Internet resources. That being said, various practical and distributive concerns make these options less than ideal.

For one thing, it is not certain that accounting mechanisms can be devised to make some of these options useful and feasible alternatives to a flat-pricing regime. The global implications of network interconnectivity are now so complex that difficulties are bound to arise in trying to establish and coordinate an international accounting system for a particular pricing policy. Further research is needed to develop appropriate electronic accounting systems for any usage-sensitive pricing mechanism.

Even if it becomes possible to implement a given access pricing system, it will have to be tested against each of the others, not just a flat-pricing regime, to determine which might prove "most efficient" under various circumstances. For now, little evidence is available to indicate that a particular mechanism might produce the best possible outcome. This is another important task for future research.

Because ISPs and backbones are private enterprises, it seems reasonable to suppose that a congestion-pricing mechanism could only be implemented if consumer demand for it was high enough. In looking at automobile traffic, one notes that even the wealthiest automobile commuters are hesitant to pay for lower travel times. This leads some to question whether there will ever be "sufficient" demand for a congestion-sensitive pricing system.[35] Indeed, a study connected with the INDEX Project has demonstrated that many

34. Winston and Shirley (1998).
35. See Calfee and Winston (1998).

consumers place very low monetary values on their time and are not willing to pay much for high-quality Internet service.[36] At face value, these results do not bode well for the widespread deployment of usage-sensitive pricing mechanisms, and further research is necessary to determine whether they reflect the general state of affairs.

Criticism can also be leveled against any sort of usage-sensitive mechanism that discriminates according to consumers' willingness to pay. Although such mechanisms may achieve an appealing outcome where efficiency is concerned, more normative policy issues (such as the "digital divide") may favor opening up the Internet to those who otherwise would not have access owing to the costs imposed by providers.[37] Finding an appropriate middle ground between these conflicting goals is likely to be one of the greatest challenges for any ISP or regulatory body involved in access provision in the coming years.

As for the question of where government and regulatory activity fits into the general picture, the more that quality Internet access becomes a scarce resource, the more potential problems there will be for competition. However, the precise nature of those problems remains uncertain, and any suppositions might prove unfounded within months of this writing. That being said, certain concerns may well crop up. As attention turns to the development of broadband access, it is important to consider the possibilities of market power on the part of both the backbone providers (see chapter 5) and

36. The INDEX project is based at the University of California at Berkeley; its objective is to identify how much consumers are willing to pay for different levels of Internet service. See Varian (1999c).

37. An alternative, less distorting, option might be to give income supplements to those who were disadvantaged and let them decide if and how to purchase access as a function of pricing and services offered.

providers of broadband services. In the case of broadband technologies, their deployment will provide service that is far superior to that of conventional "narrowband" technologies, such as standard (that is, non-DSL) copper telephone wire. As noted earlier, narrowband service provided via flat pricing may well deteriorate as the web expands to the point where standard service becomes so poor that broandband technologies are the only means of gaining "useful" access to the Internet.[38]

In such a situation, those who provide broadband services may be able to extract monopoly rents from consumers by charging greater-than-competitive prices. While many might argue that such market power will never be realized because of technological innovation and competition, it is important to consider whether competition in broadband is likely, given the extremely large start-up costs and uncertainty as to whether technology will feasibly be able to meet the ever-growing level of consumer demand for quality Internet access. In the event that only a limited number of broadband providers emerge, collusion becomes an ever more likely prospect. The possibilities for collusion, however, hinge on whether this limited number of providers would be offering homogeneous services. If different service providers were offering de facto differentiated services, then the prospects for collusion would obviously be reduced.

As with several other issues pertaining to the Internet, the overarching question is whether government intervention in access provision/pricing is appropriate. Some industry leaders have argued that the technologies and business trends associated with the Internet are changing so quickly that any attempt by the government to regu-

---

38. The prospects of service degradation of narrowband communications is obviously not a central concern of firms such as Alta Vista, and NetZero, which have begun to offer free ISP access.

late would be futile; by the time the regulations or laws are instituted, the problem(s) they were created to address would have already been dealt with by the private sector in one manner or another.
While this argument has been embraced wholeheartedly by much
of the private sector on issues such as online privacy, the industry
has not reached a clear consensus on the appropriateness of government involvement in the provision of access. Nowhere is this
tension more apparent than in the debate between ISPs and telephone and cable companies. Spurred on by the prospect of being
locked out of the broadband market, ISPs began lobbying government officials in 1999, arguing for mandated access.

AOL, for example, formed a lobbying group named openNET,
which pressed government regulators to compel broadband providers such as AT&T and Time-Warner to sell them access to their
networks.[39] After proposing to merge with Time-Warner, however,
AOL pulled back from its lobbying efforts, arguing that a market
solution was appropriate, and in February 2000 it pledged that
upon completion of the merger, the combined companies would
open Time-Warner's cable system to competing Internet service
providers.[40] Whether the government will intervene in this area
remains to be seen.

Scholars have expressed mixed views about whether competition
would be better served by letting industry hammer out the access
issues themselves or by government intervention.[41] Some favor letting the government regulate access, especially if some form of
dynamic pricing were to be introduced, to safeguard against ma-

39. Warren and White (1999).
40. Goodman (2000); Schmitt (2000).
41. For comments in favor of the former, see Kopel (1999); among those in
favor of the latter are Einhorn (1995) and Sarkar (1997).

nipulation and other anticompetitive practices.[42] In the case of broadband provision, it has been demonstrated that under a variety of assumptions about market structure mandating access to broadband facilities could enhance both consumer and broadband-provider welfare.[43] Whatever perspective the government adopts, policymakers must take into account the relative costs and network effects associated with the technologies being considered. These issues are discussed further in chapter 5.

42. Sarkar (1997) identifies the smart market proposed by MacKie-Mason and Varian (1993), in particular, as a mechanism that is ripe for abuse. In theory, those who control the system bottlenecks might be able to artificially inflate the level of network congestion in order to raise revenue. Furthermore, Sarkar argues that a smart market would require a high degree of coordination in order to function, which could not be achieved absent government intervention.

43. See MacKie-Mason (1999).

CHAPTER FOUR

ELECTRONIC COMMERCE

A TOPIC OF WIDE interest today is how the Internet is affecting traditional markets. Will the "e-marketplace"—with its lower search costs,
ease of information acquisition, and less need for conventional shelf
space—cause a boom in personalized products and mean the death
of the bricks-and-mortar retail outlet? Will the Internet have an
impact on the functions of markets, namely, to match buyers and
sellers; to facilitate the exchange of information, goods and services,
and payments; and to provide some sort of institutional infrastructure?[1] Some already consider the Internet a "nearly perfect market," whose costs and availability of information will lead to "fierce
price competition, dwindling product differentiation, and vanish-
ing brand loyalty."[2]

There is no doubt that the pricing and production of goods and
services sold over the Internet are creating an entirely new environment for consumers and merchants alike. Of course, many issues
that arise here—concerning consumer search costs and pricing
policies of online merchants, methods of packaging and selling information goods in this new environment, and the effect of infor-

1. For more on these functions, see Bakos (1998).
2. Kuttner (1998).

mation acquired by firms on prices offered to consumers—can still be addressed through conventional microeconomic theory, even more so than usual perhaps, because the Internet makes plausible assumptions that are typically considered unrealistic (such as perfect information at negligible costs). The growing literature on these issues is the subject of this chapter.

Effects of Search Costs on Pricing Policies

Many conventional economic models implicitly assume that the consumer's search costs are either negligible or nonexistent. In a market of undifferentiated goods where search costs are negligible and the usual technical assumptions are satisfied, the traditional Bertrand model of price competition would predict that goods will be priced at the marginal cost of production, and that all firms will earn zero profits. Such a result is obviously desirable to consumers, but should the traditional assumptions fail, the result might be something other than the predicted Bertrand competition equilibrium price. In considering the presence of positive search costs, several studies have derived theoretical results predicting pricing above the marginal cost.

One of the seminal works in this field, by Peter Diamond, presents a model of price determination with positive search costs.[3] Diamond's model consists of several identical firms and consumers who operate in discrete time. In each period a firm sets a price for its good, and a consumer enters only one firm. Upon entering, a consumer either makes a purchase or decides that the good is priced too high and visits another firm in the subsequent period. In every period a consumer updates his "cutoff" price (the price that induces

3. Diamond (1971).

the consumer to purchase a good in a given period rather than continue to search) as a function of his underlying demand and expectations about finding a better deal. Without analyzing the specific dynamic, Diamond assumes that consumers raise their cutoff prices between each period to correspond with a positive search cost they accrue between periods. The main insight offered by this model is that because of positive consumer search costs, firms will set an identical price that maximizes joint profits and that is greater than the competitive equilibrium. If certain assumptions are satisfied, this price will be the monopoly price.

Using Diamond's work as a starting point, several other researchers have investigated the theoretical effects of search costs on pricing dynamics. Jacques Robert and Dale Stahl examined pricing practices by firms that are able to effectively lower or eliminate search costs through the provision of informative advertising.[4] Envisioning a market of a finite number of firms selling a homogeneous good and consumers who are initially uninformed about prices but can learn prices through either searching or advertisements, Robert and Stahl asked what kinds of advertising and pricing decisions firms will make in response to consumer demands, search costs, and market structure. Given certain assumptions, they say, a unique equilibrium exists in which firms either charge a high price and do not advertise, or they charge two prices, high and low, where they advertise the low price aggressively.[5] The presence of advertising will produce heterogeneously informed consumers, and as adverting costs decrease, the equilibrium price converges to the marginal costs of production (the traditional Bertrand equilibrium).

---

4. Robert and Stahl (1993).

5. The equilibrium concept adopted by Robert and Stahl is Perfect Bayesian.

Placing their findings in the context of the Internet, one might predict that prices posted on the web will tend to be lower than those in the physical world because advertising costs, per capita, are far lower. Although this prediction seems sensible, Robert and Stahl provide another result that might conflict with this assertion: holding advertising costs constant, as search costs decrease (as one would suspect they do on the Internet), prices may still remain above marginal costs. This seemingly perverse phenomenon occurs because lower search costs actually reduce the incentive to advertise; and in doing so, they place the burden of information transmission on the consumer. Hence with (even slightly) positive search costs, Robert and Stahl's model is similar to Diamond's, in that merchants will try to raise prices as much as possible to maximize profits. It differs from Diamond's model, however, in that the ability of any one merchant to raise prices is constrained by the ability of other firms to advertise (if some firms raise their prices too much, then other firms might find it profitable to advertise, drawing all consumers to them). Since merchants on the Internet are likely to face differential advertising costs and consumer search costs are likely to be nonzero, the implications of Robert and Stahl's model for prices on the Internet are ambiguous.

Stahl also considered a different approach, ignoring advertising concerns and focusing solely on price determination in a world where consumers have varying search costs associated with shopping.[6] In this model, a finite number of stores sell identical goods, and, as in Diamond's model, consumers must visit a particular store to learn a price, and there is a reservation price that determines whether they stop their search process and purchase or continue to shop. As Stahl

6. Stahl (1996).

shows, any price between marginal cost pricing to monopoly pricing can be supported in equilibrium, depending upon the underlying distribution of consumer search costs.

In the event that no consumers enjoy shopping, the equilibrium (subgame perfect) is monopoly pricing by all firms, whereas as more shoppers' search costs converge to zero, the equilibrium price converges to marginal cost pricing.[7] For any distribution between these two extremes, however, no pure strategy equilibrium exists, and a wide range of pricing schemes might be observed. Furthermore, in considering how market structure might influence price, Stahl shows that under certain conditions (the density of shoppers being finite), the number of stores has no bearing on whether or not prices converge to marginal costs. Hence even with a substantial expansion of stores, as is being observed on the Internet, prices might not converge to the competitive equilibrium.

This small sample of the work that has been done in this area indicates there is a close relationship between consumer search costs and firm pricing practices.[8] Generally speaking, one should expect that as consumer search costs are driven down, firms will respond by lowering their prices closer to marginal costs, but many factors might constrain complete convergence. Hence in the environment of the Internet, where search costs are trivial compared with those in bricks-and-mortar outlets (mouse clicks versus car trips), one should expect electronic merchants to be lowering their prices accordingly.[9] This conjecture has spawned a number of theoretical

7. More specifically, as the density of shoppers converges to a spike around zero search costs, marginal cost pricing is realized.

8. For other discussions about the relationship between search costs and price dispersion, see Axell (1977); Rob (1985); Salop (1977); Salop and Stiglitz (1982); and Stiglitz (1987).

9. At the same time, the extent to which this generalization holds true might depend on a given consumer's knowledge about the products being consid-

and empirical investigations into the relationship between reduced transactions costs and pricing in the electronic marketplace.

Yannis Bakos, for one, examines the effects of reduced search costs on electronic marketplaces by postulating that extreme reductions in search costs might lead to the destabilization of oligopolistic pricing. This in turn might precipitate price wars, which would eliminate excess profits in a given market.[10] Building on Steven Salop's spatial competition model of differentiated products, Bakos considers a world in which sellers choose where to locate on the unit circle and consumers learn the prices and locations of given sellers for a constant cost, c.[11] Upon learning the location and product offerings for a given merchant, a consumer decides whether to purchase from a given seller or to incur search costs to look for a seller whose products and prices are more to her tastes.[12] Bakos concludes that with a large number of firms and no search costs, the equilibrium is characterized by seller profits equal to zero. Conversely, in the presence of high search costs, significant allocational inefficiencies exist. And in cases of extremely high search costs, complete market failure can ensue.

Given that extremely high search costs can cause the market to break down completely, "electronic marketplaces will enable 'missing' markets, thereby creating substantial social surplus."[13] Unem-

---

ered. In the book market, for example, if a shopper knows the title or author of a book, search costs on the Internet are trivial. Conversely, if the consumer only knows the book's subject or what its cover looks like, searching for the title on the Internet might prove difficult. Further technological innovation may eventually solve such problems, but at the moment it is difficult to say that the Internet necessarily facilitates low search costs.

10. Bakos (1997).
11. See Salop (1979).
12. The equilibrium concept adopted by Bakos is perfect Bayesian.
13. Bakos (1997: 1683).

ployment, in particular, he says, is an example in which a market (the labor market) has broken down because of the excessively high search costs associated with matching workers and employers. By lowering these search costs, perhaps by creating a job clearinghouse on the Internet (such as Monster.com), unemployment can be significantly reduced and social welfare enhanced. (As yet, however, no one has examined the effects of the introduction of such clearinghouses on unemployment rates, a topic ripe for empirical investigation.)

Besides showing how electronic marketplaces might yield benefits to buyers/consumers, Bakos investigates the corresponding incentives of sellers to invest in the development of such marketplaces. As would be expected, sellers are apt to be opposed to systems that lower buyers' search costs because such systems, in turn, would lower sellers' profits. Given that it is difficult to prevent the introduction of any sort of marketplace, Bakos suggests three courses of action that might help sellers preserve profits. First, they might try to influence the kind of system that is introduced, perhaps by requiring user fees for access to the market that would serve to compensate for lost profits. Second, sellers might want to compensate for the low cost of price information by raising the costs associated with acquiring product information, as has occurred in the airline industry. (Many airline websites will confirm that electronic marketplaces have not necessarily facilitated the diffusion of information on airline tickets). Third, sellers might seek greater differentiation between their products so that they are no longer competing with other firms over the price of identical products.

This latter possibility is consistent with the findings of Jonathan Eaton and Gene Grossman, namely, that when firms are able to choose the level of differentiation before presenting product information, the unique equilibrium will consist of firms choosing the maximum level of differentiation possible and full revelation of product information.[14] By developing products that are completely different from one another, firms avoid a vicious price competition that would eventually end in competitive pricing and zero profits for all firms. Whatever approach firms choose to take, Bakos argues, such markets will inevitably develop and once in operation will improve the economic efficiency of conventional transactions.

Using an empirical approach, Joseph Bailey examines price differences between online merchants and bricks-and-mortar stores for items such as books, compact discs, and software.[15] Noting predictions that emphasize the prospect for perfect competition on the Internet due to "frictionless" commerce following from lower transaction costs, Bailey asks whether Internet pricing policies differ from offline outlets under three assumptions. First, consistent with theoretical research, in an environment that encourages perfect competition (for example, the Internet), products should be sold at prices lower than their offline (presumably less competitive) counterparts. Second, another symptom of heightened competition would be less price variance in online versus offline prices, since online merchants should be driven to pricing close to an identical (presumably, perfectly competitive) price. Third, with heightened competition and lower menu costs, prices on the Internet are likely to change more often than in the bricks-and-mortar world, as online firms are easily able to tweak their prices in response to other firms' adjustments.

Using a database consisting of 24,000 price observations collected in February and March 1997 from fifty-two retailers, Bailey tests whether the prices of Internet and offline merchants for identical

14. Eaton and Grossman (1986).
15. See Bailey (1998a, 1998b).

products differ with respect to absolute level, dispersion, and frequency of change. Contrary to what one might suspect, only the third hypothesis, pertaining to frequency of menu adjustment, holds true across all three markets of books, compact discs, and software. Surprisingly, Internet retailers price significantly higher than physical retailers across all markets, and in two of the three markets (books and compact discs), the Internet retailers exhibit a higher level of price variance.[16] These results, Bailey claims, indicate that the Internet does not currently approximate a world of frictionless commerce and may not do so at any time in the near future.

According to Bailey, the segmentation of the market into those who do, and do not, shop online will likely lead to some form of price discrimination for a variety of products that were, up until recently, priced uniformly. Bailey therefore emphasizes the need for strong policies to protect buyers from being exploited. From an efficiency perspective, it is doubtful that the sort of price discrimination Bailey cites would necessarily reduce welfare and thus warrant government intervention.

Though Bailey's study is a solid first step toward determining whether the Internet might lead to the realization of perfect competition, clearer results might be obtained with other methods of data collection. In collecting data from offline retailers to compare with Internet seller prices, Bailey did not actually visit offline outlets but collected most of his data from the websites of bricks-and-mortar businesses. As he concedes, there is no way to confirm that the prices posted on the Internet are identical to the prices of goods in the offline outlet. If the prices on these websites were systematically lower

16. Bailey (1998a: 9) attributes the lower price variance in software prices to the fact that when the data were collected (1997), search engines for software that could easily find the lowest price were reasonably widespread, and more generally, that software tends to attract a "technically sophisticated and more demanding" consumer base.

than those in their bricks-and-mortar counterparts, it would be extremely easy to draw false inferences. One might conclude, for example, that Internet prices were not lower than offline prices, even if bricks-and-mortar prices were in fact substantially higher (but were different from those posted on their websites). A similar argument can be made with respect to the findings about price dispersion.

Erik Brynjolfsson and Michael Smith tested similar hypotheses but used a different approach to data collection.[17] To begin with, they focused only on the markets for books and compact discs: they collected pricing data for twenty books and twenty compact disc titles from eight Internet and conventional retailers. To avoid systematic bias, the offline retailers were selected at random from across the country, and validity checks were made to ensure that they were not outliers. Prices from the conventional retailers were acquired by visiting either the bricks-and-mortar outlet or its corresponding webpage after confirming that the prices posted on the webpage were identical to those of the offline outlet. A total of 8,500 prices were collected between February 1998 and May 1999.

In contrast to Bailey, Brynjolfsson and Smith found, first, that prices on the Internet are significantly lower (9 to 16 percent less) than prices for identical goods in conventional outlets. Even when accounting for shipping charges and other costs associated with purchasing either online or in stores (such as sales taxes), there is still a cost differential favoring Internet purchases. Second, depending on the measure used for price dispersion, the variance in prices is lower on the Internet than in conventional markets.[18] Like Bailey,

17. Brynjolfsson and Smith (1999).
18. The authors also discuss possible theoretical reasons for observed price dispersion. The fact that the most well-known and popular online firms (such as Amazon.com) tend to sell their products at some of the highest prices suggests reputation carries significant weight even on the Internet and might allow firms to charge above average prices when dealing in homogeneous goods.

however, Brynjolfsson and Smith found that Internet stores are far more sensitive to pricing changes than conventional stores in that Internet sellers exhibit far less "price stickiness," changing their advertised prices by significantly smaller margins than offline outlets. The authors conclude that the Internet does, in fact, help to create a world of frictionless commerce, and that as more consumers find their way online, conventional retailers will find it increasingly difficult to compete with online counterparts offering identical products.

Packaging and Pricing of Information Goods

The infrastructure of the Internet greatly reduces the costs associated with both reproducing and distributing information goods.[19] Current technologies make it possible to reproduce manuscripts and audio or video recordings that are identical in quality to the original document and to distribute them to prospective consumers instantaneously over the Internet. Extremely large databases, which may have taken years to compile, can now be distributed to virtually anyone in seconds, ready for use upon arrival. In view of the ease of replication and of altering information goods so as to "customize" them to consumer tastes, one may well ask how these products can best be packaged and priced for consumption.

The first point to note is that selling access to information goods on the Internet, such as databases or electronic newspapers, is very similar to a classic durable goods monopoly problem.[20] A seller of a given information good is able to make copies of his product that

19. See Bakos and Brynjolfsson (1999a, 1999b); Odlyzko (1996); Shapiro and Varian (1999).
20. Bulow (1982).

are identical in quality to the original, and the use of these copies (or the original) does not affect the quality of the good. This opens up the possibility of a viable secondary market. An electronic copy of the *New York Times* is not going to depreciate in quality, regardless of how many times it is read (although it may decrease in value to a given consumer). The problem for producers, then, is the classic "Coase conjecture": unless they are able to commit to a specific (finite) level of production, despite their monopoly they will be unable, in equilibrium, to price their good at anything above the marginal cost of production.[21]

Although the implications of the Coase conjecture have not yet been fully explored, several theoreticians have analyzed optimal pricing policies for producers of information goods given the unique environment of the Internet (where, for example, the marginal cost of producing information goods is close to zero). Andrew Odlyzko has hypothesized that despite declining transactions costs associated with production and sales, retailers will still be able to devise various mechanisms in order to extract consumer surplus. Chief among these mechanisms are different bundling schemes and various differential pricing strategies.[22]

When Bakos and Brynjolfsson explored how sellers might choose to package multiple information goods into one product bundle, they found that under some general conditions, bundling of multiple goods can increase efficiency.[23] If the marginal cost of copying a good is zero and certain technical assumptions about consumers' demands hold, then selling a bundle will be "remarkably superior" with respect to both producer profits and general welfare than sell-

---

21. See Coase (1972).
22. Odlyzko (1996).
23. Bakos and Brynjolfsson (1999a, 1999b, 1999c).

ing the bundled goods individually.[24] This result follows from the fact that a collective bundle is more attractive to a wider audience; hence more consumers will purchase it, and the producer will collect higher profits than if he were selling each good individually. However, these results can only be achieved if the cost of reproduction is negligible and goods that provide negative utility are not included in the bundle. Each of these conditions seems easily satisfied when the Internet is used as a sales channel.

From these results, Bakos and Brynjolfsson conclude that multigood monopolists will tend to have better profits if they bundle their goods rather than sell them individually; furthermore, single-good firms can benefit from selling their goods to a coordinating firm that will incorporate the good into their multiproduct bundle. Such findings provide economic justification for why a portal such as AOL will want to acquire many independent content providers and offer them access under the AOL banner rather than letting them fend for themselves on the open market.[25]

Drawing on the analogy of a two-period game, Bakos and Brynjolfsson also consider a model in which firms compete over both acquiring content for their bundle and selling it as a package to consumers.[26] In the first period, two firms submit bids for content, and in the second period, a good is acquired by one or both firms, depending on whether the bids were for exclusive or nonexclusive rights to the content. In equilibrium, they find, the firm that has the greater initial level of wealth will outbid the less wealthy

24. Bakos and Brynjolfsson assume that consumer valuations for goods are bounded and well-behaved, and that consumers exhibit free disposal.

25. Considering the market for software, a similar argument can be made to justify a software company's (for example, Microsoft's) practice of acquiring smaller specialized software packages from potential competitors and incorporating them into an omnibus software package.

26. Bakos and Brynjolfsson (1999b).

firm for exclusive rights to the good. Hence the wealthier bundlers will always be willing to spend more money to acquire monopoly rights over new products for their bundle. Thus for goods being bid on sequentially, the larger (wealthier) bundler will keep growing and adding more goods to its bundle as the weaker firm fails to acquire any new content.

The two-period game also applies to the downstream market for content. In the first period firms invest fixed costs into production (good acquisition), and in the second period they decide whether to offer their content as a bundle or separate products. The analytical results demonstrate the feasible ranges of costs wherein both firms will offer competing goods, and where such competition will be impossible. If certain assumptions are satisfied, unique equilibrium will occur when the firm with larger resources offers as many goods as possible in its bundle, and all consumers purchase it over either the smaller bundle, or individual products. As can also be shown, a bundler can always add profits to his bundle by adding goods, even if such goods are substitutes to existing content.

Because the marginal costs of adding more goods to the bundle are essentially zero when it consists of information goods, a potential entrant will be deterred from entering the market for a broader range of costs than would be the case under normal competition. Simply put, potential entrants either will be easily outbid in the competition for content or will lose in the downstream competition for consumers; hence they will choose to stay out of the market altogether. According to Bakos and Brynjolfsson, such entry deterrence is not the result of any threat or dynamic strategy on the part of the bundler, but simply a function of the economies of aggregation associated with the bundle. Furthermore, bundlers could plausibly enter an incumbent's market where their bundle includes the incumbent's good and force the incumbent out, because all consumers will choose to purchase the bundle over the incumbent's good. Given that bundlers will "always win" when facing either an entrant or an incumbent, incentives for innovation are significantly reduced in markets where bundling is possible. If one believes that innovation is positively related to social welfare, then these results seem to argue against the positive welfare aspects of bundling.[27]

Another important question to consider is how these bundles might be offered to consumers. More to the point, how can one ensure that pricing policies for information goods are economically viable? As programmers continue to experiment with network-based applications, users may eventually see a day when they download from a remote server via the Internet only those programs that they require at a given point in time, rather than having to buy a software package that will remain dormant on their hard drive when it is not in use. In such a world—where information goods are being rented like videotapes in a store—would the further deployment of network-based applications push retailers' profits up or down?

To assess the virtues of buying versus renting information goods, Hal Varian looks at cases in which a producer prices his product for purchase, rental, or both, as a function of consumer valuations and various transaction costs.[28] If the transaction costs of sharing the product are lower than the marginal costs of reproduction, Varian concludes, then a rental market could increase producer profits (and enhance social welfare by opening up the market to those who would not otherwise experience the good). This principle holds in the case of site licenses: it is likely to be far more costly to provide support for an additional piece of software than to share that software between users on the same networks. These economies of sharing would also seem to hold for the prospect of network-based applications, if they were ever to become commonplace.

27. Those positive aspects are discussed in Bakos and Brynjolfsson (1999c).
28. Varian (1999b).

Addressing similar questions, Peter Fishburn and his colleagues present a model of two-firm price competition for information goods when one firm sells its product for a fixed fee/subscription rate, while the other firm charges a per-use price.[29] Disregarding earlier questions about the effects of lowered transactions costs on pricing policies, the authors focus solely on how differences in pricing schemes might affect competitive equilibria. They first show that in the absence of competition, a monopolist might actually rather sell information goods through either fixed price or subscription channels than through per-use/rental agreements. The value of selling a product for a fixed price over a per-use fee will depend on the distribution of consumers' demands and the costs of product distribution. That being the case, the "population distributions for which a flat fee is most profitable are more natural" than other possible population distributions.[30]

In light of these findings, will future micropayment schemes be able to facilitate per-use consumption of information goods? If consumer demands favor owning versus renting information goods, then industry efforts aimed at developing feasible micropayment mechanisms might be for naught. Furthermore, in subsequent findings they show that even when two competing firms employ different pricing schemes, it will be difficult to avoid a price war that drives their prices down to marginal costs. One suspects that such a price war can only be avoided at the expense of one of the two firms, or in the presence of some sort of collusive arrangement, which would likely raise antitrust concerns.[31]

29. Fishburn, Odlyzko, and Siders (1997).
30. Fishburn, Odlyzko, and Siders (1997: 7).
31. Fishburn and others (1997) demonstrate that competition can lead to above marginal-cost pricing for particular functional forms of the distributions of consumers' demands. See also Fishburn and Odlyzko (1999).

Prospects for Price Discrimination

Aside from the work on technological aspects of bundling, there has been a sizable body of more traditional economic research on the relationship between product information, consumer tastes, and pricing by retailers. Some of this research has been concerned with the strategic quality of information provision by sellers as a tool for market segmentation and price discrimination. In one model, developed by Tracy Lewis and David Sappington, sellers decide how much product information to provide as a function of consumers' demands and prior expectations about product characteristics and quality.[32] The authors find that in equilibrium, firms either will provide no information about their product and sell it for the average expected price or will provide extensive information and sell only to those "high-demand" customers. The provision of product information serves to segment the market between high- and low-valuation consumers in a way that enables the sellers to post a high price that high-demand consumers will find attractive given their knowledge about the products in question.

Pricing policies are also affected by information about a firm's consumer base. As Louis Philips has argued, "markets must be separated" if price discrimination is to occur.[33] A necessary condition for price discrimination, Hal Varian agrees, is that firms must be able to "sort" customers.[34] Although firms have long been able to obtain detailed demographic information about potential (and actual) consumers from marketing research organizations, for the first time in history, the tastes of consumers can be uncovered without their being aware of it and without having to look at their purchase deci-

32. Lewis and Sappington (1994).
33. Philips (1983: 14).
34. Varian (1989: 599).

sions. For example, by employing "cookies," a firm may be able to monitor a surfer's clickstream patterns through its website and determine what products he was looking at, how long he was studying them, whether he compared prices with other items, and so on.[35] Such details, combined with demographic information, might shed light on a user's demand for a particular product and thus allow the firm in question to customize its prices accordingly, so as to maximize revenue.

According to Joseph Bailey, price discrimination is likely to occur in markets where products and services have high asset specificity.[36] For example, it is reasonable to expect "news clipping services, collaborative filtering, and other customized Internet markets" to foster the flexibility in prices that would make price discrimination possible. This is not to say that homogeneous goods are free from potential cases of discrimination. Bailey points to the case of Books.com, an Internet-based bookstore that until recently engaged in a form of third-degree price discrimination (that is, it provided different unit prices to different consumer groups).[37]

Upon visiting Books.com's website, consumers could conduct a typical search for a title, author, or subject of their choosing. Once the information was found, the Books.com price would appear along with a hyperlink for "price compare." A click on this hyperlink would call up a list of the prices for the title at Amazon.com,

35. Cookies are small programs that are placed on a user's hard drive when he visits a given site. The cookie might keep track of the user's password for a particular site, where he surfs, what he purchases, and so on. When the user returns to the site, the data stored in the cookie become available to the website, which is often customized in some way in response to the cookie (for example, the password prompt will be waived). For more information, see Galla (1998: 280–83).

36. Bailey (1998c).

37. Books.com ceased to exist on November 3, 1999, when it was acquired by Barnesandnoble.com.

Barnesandnoble.com, and Borders.com. If the Books.com price was lower than that advertised by these three, it would remain the official price; if it was not, the website would update its price to undercut the cheapest of the three and thereby establish the "new" Books.com price.[38] But this new price would not be shown if the consumer had not chosen to compare prices. In other words, Books.com was price discriminating in favor of those consumers who were more patient or price conscious, as indicated by their surfing patterns. In one sample of twenty books, the average savings from clicking on "price compare" was 15¢.[39] Following the acquisition of Books.com, Barnesandnoble.com encouraged former Books.com customers to shop at their online store by offering a one-time redeemable $10 dollar coupon for purchases larger than $25.00 at Barnesandnoble.com. The firm did not, however, adopt the price-comparing features that made Books.com a competitive threat.

Price discrimination, says Bailey, is a plausible practice for most firms on the Internet. Among the mechanisms he proposes to avoid such discrimination (at least in theory) is price competition. Another possibility is for consumers to take control of their information by prohibiting its collection or dissemination without appropriate compensation. Bailey also claims that firm reputation, generally speaking, might inhibit price discrimination. Furthermore, electronic market intermediaries (such as "shopbots") that can au-

38. On October 1, 1999, I looked up a title on social choice theory: *Positive Political Theory I: Collective Preferences and Political Analysis,* by David Austen-Smith and Jeffrey Banks. The initial Books.com price was $39.45. When I clicked on the "Price Compare" hyperlink, Books.com showed the prices of Amazon.com, Barnesandnoble.com, and Borders.com to be $39.50, $39.50, and $27.50 respectively. The "new" Books.com price was $27.20—30¢ less expensive than the closest competitor, and 31 percent off the publisher's list price ($39.50).

39. See Smith and others (1999), who also note, however, that "academics seem prone to push this button independently of price-sensitivity considerations" (fn. 10).

tomatically search the web for low prices might render price discrimination ineffective. Bailey also argues that the Federal Trade Commission has the necessary flexibility to monitor pricing practices of Internet firms and ensure that consumers are not being treated in an anticompetitive manner. Although many Internet-related cases might well fall under current FTC jurisdiction (as follows from Section 5 of the Federal Trade Commission Act and the Sherman Anti-Trust Act), it is not obvious that the practices Bailey considers would actually warrant FTC action.

Studying price discrimination in the context of lowered search costs, Jeffrey Kephart and Amy Greenwald point out that current shopbot technology could feasibly be employed to learn the posted prices on hundreds of websites simultaneously.[40] The widespread use of these programs is expected to significantly enhance competition as retailers will be forced to lower their prices constantly to ensure that a particular shopbot recognizes them as the lowest price on the market for their relevant user.[41]

To explore the effect of shopbots further, Kephart and Greenwald compare what happens when a portion of consumers do not discriminate between sellers as a function of price, and another portion are "bargain hunters" who might employ shopbots to find the lowest price possible.[42] They find that under certain assumptions and in equilibrium, only one firm will post its prices below the monopolistic price.

40. Kephart and Greenwald (1998). For a brief discussion of Internet agents, see Galla (1998: 204–07).

41. On this point, see Casey (1999); Hagel and Singer (1999); Tapscott (1996, 1998).

42. The Kephart and Greenwald model is similar in motivation to earlier models of consumer search such as those of Salop and Stiglitz (1977) and Varian (1980). In both of these models, certain consumers use search tools, such as a newspaper, to learn market prices whereas others do not. Equilibrium conditions derived in these studies are substantively similar to those of Kephart and Greenwald.

They test the robustness of this finding by simulating an economy consisting of 1,000 buyers and 5 sellers, where the sellers employ various adaptive learning mechanisms to determine their optimal prices. While the adaptive simulation results are not identical to the theoretical results for all learning algorithms, the results are consistent, in that stable marginal-cost pricing by all firms is never achieved so long as a fraction of the consumers do not employ shopbots.

In addition, the simulations suggest that in certain cases shopbots could trigger cyclical price wars and widespread monopoly pricing. Furthermore, shopbots might lead retailers to engage in a veritable "arms race" over who can lower their prices faster. That means shopbots would have to supply firms with pricing information about their competitors at tremendous speed, but the widespread and constant use of such shopbots would only serve to congest the Internet and inhibit electronic commerce. From at least one perspective, then, it seems doubtful that these emerging institutions provide obvious benefits to Internet consumers.[43]

Future of Sales Assistance

As mentioned at the outset of this chapter, one of the primary purposes of a market is to facilitate "the exchange of information."[44] That information consists of product quality and price information. In traditional transactions, sales assistants who are experts in given products are used to supply information that can facilitate a customer's decision. An important question for the sales assistance

43. Varian (1999d) speculates that the rise of price-matching devices such as shopbots will lead firms to differentiate their products on grounds other than price. Some likely forms of differentiation are consumer-specific versions of a given product, as well as loyalty programs for shopping with a given merchant.

44. See Bakos's (1998) remarks about the functions of a market.

sector of the economy is whether it will continue to be viable in the face of declining transaction costs associated with information acquisition on the Internet.

To investigate the need for expertise and assistance in markets, Birger Wernerfelt develops a model in which buyers and sellers engage in a sequential "matching game" over product qualities and prices.[45] In the first period, a seller learns the types of products he has available for sale. In the second stage a buyer communicates his preferences. In the third stage the seller identifies the proper match for the buyer and makes a take-it-or-leave it offer for the product. In the last period, the buyer accepts or rejects the offer. The relevant information for matching can be communicated in a number of ways (printed brochures, salesperson monologue, dialogue, and the like). The costs associated with each vary.

Under certain assumptions, Wernerfelt shows, the dialogue between seller and buyer can lead to the most efficient outcome (with respect to both cost and product matching). Furthermore, with respect to active sales assistance more generally, sales assistance appears more likely to thrive as an institution where products are varied and possibly complicated, buyers tend to have little technical knowledge, and the cost of a sales assistant's time is lower than the buyers' cost.[46] It is hard to imagine a complete migration of all goods and services to the automated selling environment of the Internet under such conditions. For certain products, even though information acquisition will be reasonably costless, a consumer might still require input from an expert or sales assistant to ensure that she is making appropriate purchase decisions.

45. Wernerfelt (1994).
46. Wernerfelt also argues that sales assistance is likely to thrive in industries where unpleasant buying experiences can significantly influence future purchase decisions and in cases where institutions can be created to give strong long-term incentives to sales representatives.

The interesting question for Gary Biglaiser is how markets for durable goods will encourage the institution of the middleman. "Middleman" in this instance refers to any intermediary who purchases a durable good from one individual and sells it to another buyer, without changing it or affecting its value in any de facto manner. A typical example would be a used-coin salesman who buys and sells coins without actually altering the material value of the coin in any way. Without some credible signal of quality for a given product, of course, the market for durable goods will quickly collapse into the market for lemons.[47] In certain markets, Biglaiser argues, a qualified middleman known for his expertise can serve to enhance aggregate welfare by providing just such a signal (thereby resolving the adverse selection problem).

If a middleman exists, Biglaiser finds, market segmentation will ensue in equilibrium, in that all high-quality goods will pass through the middleman whereas all low-quality goods will be sold on the open market from owner to buyer. Furthermore, in such a regime the middleman will receive a high enough price for his services that he will not cheat his customers by selling goods of low quality or at inappropriate prices. Finally, these results will still hold even if the investment required by the middleman to establish his credibility as an "expert" is extremely high. Moreover, middlemen can be expected to show up wherever many low-quality goods are being traded and there is a large difference in quality between high- and low-quality goods, although it is difficult to discern relative quality levels from casual inspection.

---

47. See Akerloff (1970). Because buyers cannot differentiate between "high-" and "low-quality" goods, owners of high-quality products, knowing that they will be unable to sell their good for its market value, will refuse to enter the market, leaving only goods of low quality (lemons) in the market.

Such conclusions seem to suggest that, absent any sort of inter-mediation, widespread person-to-person sales are not likely to take place via the Internet, at least not for certain types of goods. After all, how many people would feel comfortable buying rare coins or stamps from a collector without being able to examine them in per-son? Anticipating such problems, intermediary institutions have begun to enter Internet-based collectible markets. Collectible base-ball cards, for instance, pass through an inspection before being posted for sale on the web. Independent agencies grade the cards, encase them in plastic, and affix a stamp indicating the grade and grading house. Such a process guarantees that the cards being sold conform to some agreed-upon standard by collectors, so that they can attract fair-market prices, independent of personal inspection.

A similar evolution of intermediaries is being reported in empiri-cal studies. When Bailey and Bakos compared the market activities of thirteen firms engaged in electronic commerce involving infor-mation goods with those of retailers in conventional goods, they found a distinct difference in certain intermediary roles.[48] In cases such as product aggregation and certain infrastructure-related ac-tivities, the roles were significantly diminished in electronic market settings. While these functions seem to fall by the wayside, however, it seems that there is still a great, if not greater, need for intermedi-ary services to create consumer trust, and, in some cases, to facili-tate matching between buyers and sellers. Although this was a preliminary analysis and should be interpreted with caution, the trends uncovered seem to support theoretical results indicating that intermediaries will remain viable in electronic markets.[49]

48. Bailey and Bakos (1997).
49. See Biglaiser (1993); Wernerfelt (1994).

Summary and Implications

So far, the research on electronic commerce suggests that the Internet will have a significant long-run effect on the way commercial transactions take place. But what will happen once electronic markets mature? Will lower search costs and price-matching policies lead to something approximating marginal-cost pricing? Will the ease of monitoring firms' pricing policies necessarily bring on vigorous competition? And will firms be able to engage in price discrimination by more sophisticated methods than those exhibited by Books.com as they become better educated about their consumer base?

Theoretical analyses offer no firm conclusions about how lowered search costs will affect consumer prices in the long run. As this chapter has shown, information-based pricing models can justify pricing policies that range from marginal cost to monopoly levels. Because many models fail to distinguish between the various categories of information and advertising (prices, products, firm reputation, and the like), it is difficult to say how decreasing search costs will affect each of these elements (and their interactions), not to mention prices.

Empirical evidence is mixed as to whether marginal-cost pricing will ever be achieved. Although certain markets on the Internet have lower prices and less price dispersion, this does not seem to be a general phenomenon.[50] Some findings about price dispersion are not robust to various specifications, and evidence from other markets might add to the skepticism. In the market for airline tickets, for instance, prices offered online can differ by as much as 18–28 percent, depending on how one controls for qualitative differences

50. See Brynjolfsson and Smith (1999).

in the tickets.[51] The evidence regarding absolute price differences between the online and offline world is also sketchy. In the Japanese used-car auction market, for one, price levels are consistently higher in electronic markets than offline auction blocks.[52]

Faced with the empirical realities of persistent high prices and price dispersion, one must ask what might be generating these outcomes. In markets for homogeneous goods, such pricing patterns would seem to suggest that reputation is a likely cause.[53] Note that customers who regularly employ shopbots will persist in purchasing from retailers such as Amazon.com that post consistently higher prices than their shopbot findings. While Amazon.com might not have the lowest prices, it is well known for its prompt delivery practices and is widely accepted as a legitimate business actor. It is these qualities that might be driving transactions.

On the web, a transaction medium that by construction is almost devoid of personal contact, it seems likely that intangible qualities such as brand recognition could define consumers' demands more so than price. Hence a firm with a high-quality brand name might have the luxury of consistently pricing above most of its competitors because it recognizes that consumers will still choose to shop with it as opposed to its lower priced competitors.[54] New firms can

51. See Clemons, Hann, and Hitt (1999). Although Clemons and his colleagues do not compare these prices with offline counterparts, "the amount of dispersion they find is higher than one might expect," according to Smith and others (1999).

52. Lee (1998).

53. See Smith and others (1999). However, Clemons and his colleagues (1999) attribute the observed price dispersion to concerted efforts to engage in price discrimination, in conjunction with differing degrees of product differentiation, rather than any sort of reputation effect per se.

54. The empirical implication of such a theory is that the more well-known online retailers will consistently price higher than the less well-known retailers. Brynjolfsson and Smith (1999) show that this trend holds at least in the market for books.

then be expected to try to establish brand name and firm reputation by such means as aggressive advertising and free promotions in an effort to expand market share and be able to charge higher prices commensurate with the reputations gained. Closely related to the value of a brand name are the actual pecuniary benefits that a consumer accrues by continuing to shop with a particular retailer. Various loyalty programs such as discounts for repeat shoppers can serve to "lock in" prospective consumers with particular retailers.[55] Once locked in, retailers will have some (albeit possibly limited) latitude with which to exercise market power.[56]

While firm reputation and loyalty programs might prevent widespread convergence in prices, price-matching policies can serve to stimulate the "race to the bottom." Whether such policies might actually enhance consumer welfare is an open question. Some think that price-matching might harm consumers by facilitating collusion, whereas others believe that in some cases it can unambiguously enhance consumer welfare.[57] Still others believe collusion is likely to occur because of certain features particular to the Internet.[58]

First, as noted earlier, price-matching, if conducted by shopbots, could lead to the unpleasant externality of Internet congestion.[59] Therefore, if all firms are trying to match each other by using

55. For example, while it existed, Books.com rewarded "bookmark points" to customers for every dollar spent at the website, which could be redeemed for discounts toward future purchases. On such programs, see Shapiro and Varian (1999); Varian (1999d).

56. The validity of this statement necessarily rests on the requirement that the prices being charged by a given firm trying to exercise "market power" are still less than the costs to a consumer of switching and forgoing the benefits of the respective firm's loyalty program.

57. Corts (1996).

58. Salop (1986: 271) cites price-matching and meeting-competition clauses specifically as a practice that can "facilitate oligopolistic co-ordination."

59. Kephart and Greenwald (1998).

shopbots, the entire web might suffer at times. Hence it is inappropriate to say that consumers will "benefit" from widespread price-matching.[60] Second, given that monitoring costs on the Internet are negligible, this could facilitate efforts to coordinate prices. If the field of Internet retailers of homogeneous goods shrinks to only a few, it seems plausible that price coordination might emerge, using shopbots as a monitoring device, to keep prices set just above the point at which widespread migration to bricks-and-mortar outlets is prevented.[61]

Views about how prospects for price discrimination might affect consumer welfare also seem to be mixed. On one hand, price discrimination can be shown to enhance welfare in certain situations by expanding the potential market for certain products. In the case of information goods in particular, the Internet could easily facilitate the practice of "versioning" products, or selling identical goods of varying quality (also known as "damaged goods").[62] That could lead to a substantial expansion of the potential consumer base and thus enhance aggregate welfare. On the other hand, if firms implement price discrimination by tying lower prices to delay (longer search processes, hunting through numerous menus, and the like), then welfare effects are ambiguous.[63] For certain cases, the outcome is socially inferior to a competitive outcome.

60. Of course, the plausibility of the claim that shopbot proliferation will clog up the Internet is an empirical question that requires further study. Simulation exercises might help determine whether this is a realistic possibility.

61. One would expect cyclical price wars to be associated with such coordination as firms that attempted to defect and lower prices were quickly detected and then punished. Thus it would be interesting to investigate whether the prices of the larger online retailers (for the book market: Amazon.com, Barnesandnoble.com, and Borders.com) exhibit such a pattern.

62. Shapiro and Varian (1999); Varian (1999d). On damaged goods, see Deneckere and McAfee (1996).

63. Chiang and Spatt (1982).

Welfare effects aside, greater price discrimination invites more lawsuits alleging discrimination. Currently, business-to-business transactions on the Internet account for a substantial portion of electronic commerce. Estimates for total business-to-business transactions range from 40 percent to 80 percent of all commerce conducted on the web.[64] While price discrimination from business to end-consumers is not illegal per se, suppliers discriminating between retailers or secondary suppliers could be violating the Robinson-Patman Act. With the technological innovations discussed in this chapter, it seems likely that primary suppliers will be better informed about their consumer base than ever before and hence be able to extract differential rents from customers as a function of their willingness to pay. In the event that the customers are competitors in a secondary market, the retailer could be subject to antitrust liability.

Concerns about competition may also arise in the bundling of content and services. Although bundling may provide various efficiencies, such positive aspects may not compensate for anti-competitive concerns raised earlier in this chapter. The recent Department of Justice case against Microsoft points to only one instance in which bundling can become a point of contention between industry and regulators. As more firms seek to offer wider and better-integrated services to attract users, questions will arise as to whether the provision of such goods serves to weaken competition.

A number of Internet retail firms that originally specialized in particular products have already expanded their spheres of interest well beyond their original content in an effort to secure their position as a premier "one-stop-shopping" site. Amazon.com, for example, has expanded beyond books to music, videos, toys, and auctions. In an attempt to establish itself as an online shopping mall,

---

64. Goolsbee and Zittrain (1999); Cline and Neubig (1999b).

it has formed partnerships with different businesses to offer products ranging from pet toys to hardware to Rolex watches. Although large content-providers and online shopping malls might enhance consumer welfare by offering a wider range of options, exclusion and other (possibly) anticompetitive practices will undoubtedly command the attention of antitrust agencies.[65]

As electronic commerce matures and more data become available, future research needs to move in several directions. First, it would be important to determine whether the price differences (or lack thereof) between online and offline firms could become a robust phenomenon across all markets. In the event that certain markets still exhibit higher online prices, one might ask what different markets might facilitate a price differential favoring bricks-and-mortar outlets. It is not obvious a priori that all industries will necessarily want to migrate to the web as soon as possible. Although online firms may experience significant cost-savings with respect to inventory and physical plant maintenance, other costs—especially for computer and Internet technical support—can become quite cumbersome. As firms such as Recreational Equipment Inc. (REI.com) have demonstrated, skilled labor is sorely needed to maintain the online web side of the business. This demand has led to consistent increases in operating expenses, making them even higher than at bricks-and-mortar outlets in some cases.[66]

Future research across industries might also focus on transactions involving large-ticket items such as automobiles and consumer

65. At the same time, it is possible that a limited number of online shopping sites or portals might never become dominant. Such dominance is more likely to arise if users consistently surf to a limited number of sites. This is an empirical question about surfer retention, of course, and deserves further examination. Investigating these issues, Adar and Huberman (1999) suggest various strategies that firms might employ on their websites to help retain surfers.

66. Kaufman (1999).

electronics, where repeat buying is less frequent (or there is a long period between purchases) than in the case of books or compact discs. For such items, loyalty programs, for example, should not affect consumer choice, so it would be interesting to learn whether lower search costs do in fact lead to lower prices.

Note, too, that prices on the Internet might not even accurately reflect the welfare benefits that consumers receive from shopping online. When one takes into account the convenience associated with delivery and the appeal of customized orders, consumers may still be better off purchasing products online. Future research might explore this perspective by developing welfare measures that accurately reflect consumers' web experiences and that do not solely rely on product price data. These very issues are currently under investigation at the Internet Policy Institute, in collaboration with the Brookings Institution.[67]

Researchers also need to examine the extent to which the ability of firms to engage in price matching facilitates de facto collusion. By programming a shopbot to collect pricing data from several stores (either small or large items), one can easily compile a rich database with which to discern pricing patterns that might suggest price coordination or retaliation for deviations from a price agreement.

Yet another topic that merits attention is whether the Internet is serving as an effective clearinghouse for hard-to-move durable goods. Given the information-rich environment of the Internet, one might expect certain goods to be sold more often on the web than in the real world, as more and more interested consumers become better informed about the potential product offerings available on the Internet. The market for secondhand goods, in particular, might flow more freely on the Internet than in the offline world, as con-

67. See Internet Policy Institute (1999).

sumers would no longer be limited to product choices in local markets. Consistent with this notion, websites such as Yardsale.com and
"Perfect Yardsale" (introduced by Priceline.com) emerged in early
2000 to facilitate online secondhand markets for everyday products
that would conventionally be sold through garage sales.[68] Compari-
sons between sales from online secondhand markets such as auction sites and "yard sale" sites and sales through classified ads or
secondhand specialty stores (disregarding the middleman problem
for a moment) would help clarify whether the Internet truly facilitates "frictionless commerce."

---

68. Groer (2000).

CHAPTER FIVE

NETWORK EFFECTS

WITH THE RAPID expansion of electronic commerce, almost no word has become as commonplace as "networks." The literature on Internet-related business strategy alone is rife with topics ranging from "creating an information age business network" to how managers can "leverage network effects" in order to increase returns to scale.[1] Virtually everyone seems to sense that networks are important in today's economy. While the terms "network," "network effects," and "network externalities" are being used interchangeably, their meaning is not entirely clear. Equally puzzling is the way in which network structure might affect the Internet and electronic commerce.

According to one definition, a network is "a set of nodes connected, directly or indirectly, by a set of links" and marked by the presence of "network externalities."[2] A good is said to possess network externalities if its value to an individual user increases as more individuals use it. The concept of network externalities, in discussing the Internet, has gained attention because of its association with "Metcalfe's Law" (named after Bob Metcalfe, the inventor of the

---

1. See Mendelson and Ziegler (1999: 100); Hagel and Armstrong (1997: 44).
2. Schmalensee (1995).

Ethernet).[3] This law states that the value of a given network is proportional to the square of the number of its users.

The most straightforward example of a product having network effects is a communications network such as a phone system or a fax machine: with only one user, it is basically worthless, but as more people come to own phones or faxes, the value of the system and the consumer demand associated with it increase significantly. Network effects can be divided into direct and indirect effects.[4] An example of a direct effect is exhibited with a communications network: the more people who become part of the network, the more people one can communicate with, and hence the more valuable the network is to a given user. An example of an indirect effect is observed with products such as consumer electronics technology and computer systems. As more individuals purchase compact disc (CD) players or a given operating system, suppliers of technological complements (CDs or software) recognize the rise in value associated with the network and increase the production of these necessary components accordingly.[5]

The value of a given communications network such as a phone system rests on the fact that all phones use a common communications standard that enables any member of the network to communicate with another member.[6] This could also apply to the Internet,

3. Shapiro and Varian (1999: 184).

4. See Farrell and Saloner (1985); Katz and Shapiro (1986).

5. Shapiro and Varian (1999) present examples of success and failure stories about various products (such as Betamax standard videotapes and ATMs) that possessed network effects and whose markets expanded or contracted on the basis of consumer expectations about the future size and scope of the network associated with the good. In contrast, Liebowitz and Margolis (1994) argue that the failure of many products, the Betamax standard in particular, might have been due to poor management decisions rather than any sort of network effects.

6. Varian (1999d).

as the communications protocol (TCP/IP) serves as a de facto open standard between completely disparate networks, allowing members from different networks to connect with one another without actually belonging to one another's networks. In allowing such interconnection, the Internet truly serves as a "network of networks." That being said, one should expect the conventional economic principles that apply to networks to also apply to the Internet, whether one is considering interconnection agreements, technological innovation, or electronic commerce more generally.

The role of network effects in the context of the Internet has received little attention in the literature. As this chapter points out, most studies focus on subjects such as network effects in technology adoption, strategic pricing policies by firms, and efficient network size. Even then, many treat network effects and emerging information technology more generally. As a result, this discussion concentrates on the traditional literature on technology innovation, along with some Internet and technology-related matters.[7]

Network Effects and Technology Adoption

An early study of note, by Jeffrey Rohlfs, posits that for a generic "communications system," the utility of a given subscriber increases as more users are added to the network.[8] Rohlfs endeavors to determine the equilibrium user set associated with such a network and to identify the conditions under which such an equilibrium can be

7. The body of literature dealing with "network effects" is quite broad. Only a minute portion is discussed in this chapter. For a more extensive treatment of the subject, with a list of relevant references, see Tirole (1988), particularly chapter 10. Economides (1996), and Katz and Shapiro (1994) also provide detailed overviews on the literature pertaining to the economic issues surrounding networks and vertically related industries.

8. Rohlfs (1974).

achieved.[9] Employing a very general framework, Rohlfs finds that for any given price, many equilibria may emerge; and the realization of a given equilibrium is determined, in part, by the size of the initial network. In other words, the "viability" of a given equilibrium is a function of the initial network size. If the number of initial users is "large" enough (as defined by the theoretical results), then the system is said to possess "critical mass" and is guaranteed to eventually converge to an equilibrium user set. Conversely, if the initial user set is below critical mass, the equilibrium will not be realized.

Building on this distinction between potential and realized equilibria, Rohlfs suggests several strategies that firms (or other service providers) might employ to solve the "start-up problem" to ensure that critical mass is achieved. One possibility would be to give the product away or offer it to potential users for a low introductory price.[10] In addition, Rohlfs states that the presence of small communities or interest groups can help ameliorate the difficulties associated with achieving critical mass (assuming that the communities adopting the product en masse are large enough, in the aggregate, to achieve critical mass).

The theoretical plausibility of Rohlfs's pricing strategies is assessed by Louis Cabral, David Salant, and Glen Woroch through an analysis of pricing policies that might be employed by a monopolist producing a good with network effects.[11] Cabral and his colleagues

9. Rohlfs (1974: 17) defines the equilibrium user set simply as "the set of users consistent with all individuals' (users and nonusers) maximizing their utilities."

10. Rohlfs (1974) recognizes that inefficiencies are likely to follow the implementation of a single low introductory price, as low-valuation consumers are likely to drop out of the network as the price is raised following widespread adoption. In order to ensure that the equilibrium user set is realized, Rohlfs proposes price discrimination as a possible solution.

11. Cabral, Salant, and Woroch (1997).

attempt to determine whether the Coase conjecture will always hold
for durable goods: whether the price posted to first-period consumers is necessarily higher than any price posted for subsequent periods. They consider cases in which consumers are "small" and "large"
with respect to their influence on the network. In certain instances,
they find that the presence of network externalities can facilitate
penetration pricing, wherein prices for new products are lowest at
their time of introduction, even in the absence of any sort of competition. This result confirms Rohlfs's suspicions that such strategies may help firms develop a viable installed base. Consistent with
this revelation, the authors note that their findings provide a theoretical explanation for the pricing trends at CompuServe and
Prodigy, two Internet service providers that were priced lowest upon
their debut and then consistently increased to a stable plateau as
more members subscribed to their services.

Michael Katz and Carl Shapiro, along with Joseph Farrell and
Garth Saloner, examine similar issues in a competitive setting. They
are particularly interested in technology adoption in various markets where network effects are present.[12] Katz and Shapiro present
a static model of oligopolistic competition where consumers' utilities for a given product are explicitly defined as a function of its
price, the "types" of consumers, and the number of consumers who
use the product.[13] In this model firms decide how much of their
product to produce and whether to make it technologically compatible with other products. The equilibrium concept employed is
"fulfilled expectations Cournot equilibrium" (FECE), which implies
that a given firm chooses its output level on the belief that consum-

---

12. Katz and Shapiro (1985, 1986); Farrell and Saloner (1985, 1986). For a
nontechnical discussion of various strategies that firms might employ in standard setting competitions, see Besen and Farrell (1994).

13. Katz and Shapiro (1985).

ers' expectations about the network sizes are common knowledge, and competing firms' outputs are fixed.[14] Like Rohlf, they find that multiple equilibria may be realized, under certain conditions regarding consumers' expectations about potential network size. Hence the likelihood of any given network becoming the dominant standard is a self-fulfilling prophecy, the outcome depending on whether consumers believe that the standard's dominance is plausible.

Katz and Shapiro also examine a firm's strategic choice about whether to institute compatibility with other firms. As might be expected, firms that are large and have a strong consumer base will not favor compatibility as much as firms with weaker consumer bases, regardless of social welfare considerations. Under certain conditions, widespread industry compatibility may enhance welfare over incompatibility, and institutions such as side payments between firms and industry coalitions may foster such compatibility. Although these mechanisms may have adverse effects (in the form of competition-chilling cartels, for instance), the authors argue for antitrust exemptions where industry "cartels" are likely to yield welfare-enhancing compatibility decisions for their products.

In another study, Katz and Shapiro assess a similar two-period model in which consumers must choose between two incompatible technologies, either of which may be sponsored.[15] A technology is "sponsored" if a producer has proprietary rights over the technology, such as a patent, that might allow him to price the product at

14. Unlike a Bertrand competition game in which firms strategically choose prices subject to a demand function that varies according to price, conventional Cournot competition models have firms strategically choosing quantities subject to a price function that varies according to total quantity available on the market.

15. Katz and Shapiro (1986).

something other than competitive levels. If neither technology is sponsored, both technologies, it seems, will be subject to marginal-cost pricing, and (not surprisingly) because of the existing network externalities, the competitive equilibrium will likely be inefficient from a social welfare standpoint. This outcome changes dramatically, however, when one or both technologies are sponsored. When one technology is sponsored, the sponsoring firm might be able to create a solid established base in the first period by engaging in below-cost penetration pricing that will allow its technology to become the dominant standard in the second period.[16] While such standardization might prove optimal over the competitive outcome, sponsorship could yield suboptimal outcomes, note Katz and Shapiro, in that the "wrong" technology can be adopted from a social welfare standpoint.[17] As for cases in which both technologies are sponsored, the rational expectations of consumers can lead to a normatively desirable outcome: the technology that would be superior in future periods is made the standard, despite a cost differential that favors an inferior technology in the current period.

An important question for Farrell and Saloner is how likely are new standards or technologies (such as different formats for digitized music) to displace entrenched products in cases where there is an incompatible installed base?[18] To answer this question, the authors construct models in which users (either users of old technology, or those who are altogether new to the market) must choose

16. These results are similar to those of Rohlfs (1974) and Cabral and others (1997).

17. This somewhat perverse result arises possibly because the sponsoring firm might price its technology so far below cost in the first period that all first-period consumers adopt it. If the size of the first period network is sufficiently large, second-period consumers will also adopt the sponsored technology even if it is priced higher than the unsponsored technology and less desirable.

18. Farrell and Saloner (1986).

whether to adopt a new technology. If those choosing the technology are new users, equilibria exist where the new technology both is and is not adopted as the dominant standard. Here, the results imply that the primary factors behind the decision to adopt the new technology are the size of the installed base that favors the old technology and the perceived benefits of the new network. Though this is not a general property of products with network effects, cases can be found in which the installed base of the old technology can be viewed as a barrier to entry.

If installed bases can dissuade entry, Farrell and Saloner note, both incumbent and entrant firms might take certain, arguably anticompetitive, steps to either bring a new technology to market or to keep a competitor out of the market altogether. From the perspective of the incumbent producing the old technology, various "predatory" pricing schemes might be an effective way to expand their installed base to prevent entry of the new technology. Interestingly, these predatory pricing schemes, while preventing the entry of a competitor, could plausibly fail conventional tests of predatory practices.[19] Suppose that the incumbent firm is a monopolist, and upon witnessing an entrant trying to bring his technology to market, he drops his price below the monopoly price but still keeps it above marginal-cost pricing. Now suppose that this price cut causes his installed base to expand substantially, with the result that entrants cannot penetrate the market at a viable scale. After preventing entry, the incumbent could raise his prices again, to the monopoly level. Although such a situation is arguably anticompetitive, it cannot be accounted for by the conventional standards for predation because the incumbent is still pricing above average variable cost, and reentry costs are irrelevant.

19. See Areeda and Turner (1975); Ordover and Willig (1981).

For their part, entrants might attempt to stall the expansion of the incumbent's installed base by preannouncing their technology before it is actually released. New users, anticipating the potential benefits of such a technology, might choose to wait for its release rather than accept the current standard. Hence new technologies might be adopted where they might not have been if such an announcement had not been made. Such preannouncements might reduce social welfare, however, in the sense that the welfare loss experienced by those consumers stranded with old technologies might be far larger than the welfare gains accruing to consumers who adopt the new technology.

Disregarding market competition, Farrell and Saloner also ask when network externalities are likely to leave industries stranded with old standards that are inferior to new technologies.[20] They consider a model of adoption in which N firms make a discrete, sequential choice about whether to adopt a new technology. The answer to this question, the authors find, hinges on the amount of information available to the firms at the time of their decision. Where the information is complete and perfect and firms are fully aware of the relative payoffs to all industry players who adopt a particular new technology, in equilibrium all firms in the industry will switch to a new superior technology, if such a technology is available. Hence there will be no "excess inertia."[21] Not surprisingly, where information is incomplete and firms are thus less certain about industry-switching dynamics, equilibria can arise when the industry fails to adopt a new technology, despite the fact that such adoption would be best for society (Pareto optimal). If communication takes place

20. Farrell and Saloner (1985).

21. "Excess inertia" refers to the phenomenon in which the entire industry would prefer to switch to a new technology but fails to do so. See Farrell and Saloner (1985).

before an adoption decision is made, the outcome tends to be more stable and efficient industry adoption prevails. This implies, once again, that market coordination might not necessarily be a bad thing from a social welfare standpoint.[22] If, as many say, current market conditions reflect an incomplete information environment, such results imply a potential for stranding in the Internet.[23]

Applications to the Internet

Much of the research on network effects has implications for the strategies that firms might try to employ in bringing their products to the Internet market and establishing their "installed base." If many of these strategies turn out to be anticompetitive in the environment of the Internet, as appears plausible, do they warrant the attention of the government and antitrust agencies? The first point to make in answering this question is that it may be difficult to find network effects that are unique to the Internet. That is, many of the Internet-based applications that seem clear candidates for having network externalities (such as shared databases) have bricks-and-mortar counterparts that exhibit many of the same properties. Therefore the following discussion of implications for the Internet necessarily applies to conventional network industries as well.

One of the more likely venues for anticompetitive problems is the Internet infrastructure. According to Lawrence White, "Even if competition is present in most of the components of a network,

22. The equilibrium concept adopted in deriving this latter finding is Perfect Bayesian.

23. This point should not be overstated. As noted by Katz and Shapiro (1994: 108), "There is no general result implying excess inertia in market equilibria." Because of the existence of multiple equilibria, it is impossible to objectively determine the conditions under which a particular market or industry may become "stranded."

monopoly in just a single component may be sufficient to capture all the potential rents from the transactions that use that component."[24] For a parallel situation in the Internet environment, consider the current state of interconnection agreements between regional networks and backbone providers.

While most backbones currently do not charge for network connection between one another, a fee is usually levied for each connection from backbone to regional networks, and the smaller networks appear to have limited bargaining power in these transactions.[25] Given that the backbone owners arguably possess an essential facility in the conventional sense, several competitive concerns may affect the prospects for infrastructure development. First, as backbone owners begin to provide integrated services, such as acting as an ISP to end-users, competition may well dwindle because backbone providers could raise interconnection fees so high that they prevent potential competitors for ISP services from entering the market. Although such a scenario may seem plausible, theoretical studies suggest that backbone providers are more likely to engage in some manner of price discrimination to "squeeze" as much value as possible from those firms that must rely on their technologies.[26]

Regardless of which situation is more likely, these issues have some real-world bite. Network interconnection fees and possible service

24. White (1999: 14–15).

25. A substantial body of work dealing with the economics and technical details surrounding settlements and interconnection agreements on the Internet overlaps with the topics discussed in chapter 3. For a treatment of such issues, see Bailey (1997); Herzog, Shenker, and Estrin (1997); Lehr and Weiss (1996); and Srinagesh (1997).

26. See Economides and Woroch (1992); Ordover and Willig (1981, 1999). Of course, any sort of "squeeze" may require some price coordination on the part of the backbone providers.

degradation became major concerns surrounding the 1999 MCI-WorldCom merger because the combined firm would have clearly been a dominant backbone provider. To avoid litigation, MCI divested its Internet business to a third party, thereby preserving a "rough parity" among existing backbone providers.[27] Future cases may have a different outcome: the theoretical possibilities for price discrimination may require relevant agencies to take some sort of antitrust action.[28]

Price discrimination at the bottlenecks is not the only problem likely to draw the attention of antitrust authorities. Standardization, Mark Lemley claims, creates a number of potential problems for the Internet.[29] The inherent network externalities associated with the Internet, combined with the value of product interoperability and the presence of notable resource commitments on the part of investors and consumers, make some level of standardization inevitable. Furthermore, this standardization will likely give rise to natural monopolies, providing one group of widely adopted products "with market durability that may significantly outlast the competitive superiority of the products."[30] The software industry is not a natural monopoly per se, Lemley argues, but its natural tendencies toward standardization, combined with consumers' expectations about market position, may render competition somewhat inefficient.

For Lemley, the possibility that consumers might be harmed in a "winner-take-all" battle for standards should motivate consumers and

27. Melamed (1999); Robinson (1999).

28. Unlike the matters covered in chapter 4, however, any price discrimination that might occur in relation to backbone providers and regional networks would not be subject to Robinson-Patman enforcement because Robinson-Patman applies only to markets for tangible goods and is not relevant for service provision, such as backbone access.

29. Lemley (1996).

30. Lemley (1996: 1052).

industry alike to ensure that competing standards are interoperable. Such interoperability might be achieved through existing intellectual property laws, government mandate, or industry-wide adoption of a universal standard.[31] By way of example, the private sector has obviously been successful in navigating the standard-setting minefield in the area of basic communication protocol. With the impending introduction of technologies such as network-based applications, however, many questions are likely to arise over which standards to adopt for operating systems and to ensure that such applications function efficiently on the Internet. In this kind of situation, Lemley would argue, it would be imprudent to "condemn" industry standard-setting coalitions that often raise red flags for regulators. Such organizations could indeed foster anticompetitive cartels, says Lemley, but the benefits of information sharing and of reaching an industry consensus might ameliorate the usual anticompetitive concerns.[32]

Exclusivity provisions in networks may be another source of antitrust concerns, because of the ease with which market power can be established in relation to normal goods.[33] According to David Balto, exclusivity provisions could have the anticompetitive effects of foreclosing new entrants, in that they raise another barrier to entry in a given industry.[34] Foreclosure could stifle innovation, as entrenched

31. Lemley (1996) notes that complications exist with all of these options, ranging from government ignorance about the relevant technologies to the possibility of industry-group coercion on the part of a dominant firm.

32. These are the same benefits pointed out by Katz and Shapiro (1985).

33. Balto (1999); Shapiro (1999).

34. Balto (1999). An example of such exclusivity might arise in a joint venture where the members agree not to compete with the network, either by themselves or as participants in alternate networks. Balto cites the Florist Telegraph Delivery Association (FTD) as an example of a network that has employed such an exclusivity provision.

market leaders would not feel the competitive pressure to offer new products to maintain industry dominance. To prevent such harm, antitrust authorities need to devote attention to market definition and de facto market power, recognizing that even a small installed base might enable a firm to become far more entrenched than it otherwise would be, absent the presence of network effects.

This issue has already generated debate in the context of the Internet, most notably in relation to standards for digital music downloads. In 1998 a recording industry consortium known as the Secure Digital Music Initiative launched a push for uniform standards.[35] One could imagine that if members of this coalition (hypothetically) agreed to certain protocols and standards but chose not to make the applications available to all music producers, such actions could well yield anticompetitive effects warranting government attention. Similar coordination efforts are occurring in the market for digital books, where industry representatives have been attempting to develop uniform standards for digitizing text for Internet transmission.[36]

Another standard-setting competition began in the fall of 1999, when AOL and Microsoft entered into a debate over Instant Messenger networks. Microsoft, hoping to make its messaging service the dominant network, tried to provide its 4.5 million Microsoft Network (MSN) members with access to AOL's Instant Messenger service so that MSN members could communicate with AOL's members.[37] To maintain the exclusivity of its standard, AOL began blocking MSN's attempts at compatibility. After developing more than two dozen versions of its Messenger software, each of which was successfully blocked, Microsoft gave up in November 1999, citing

35. Richtel (1999).
36. Macavinta (1999).
37. Chandrasekaran (1999a).

concerns about security as the reason. Despite their drawn-out conflict, both AOL and Microsoft pledged to develop a compatible protocol for their two systems to ensure interoperability.

Other issues that may merit government intervention have to do with universal access. As already noted, a given technology or system can only become dominant if there is a sufficient number of users to reach that "critical mass." Now that the educational and economic benefits of Internet access are being loudly hailed, a question has arisen—as in earlier debates about telephony—about whether the government should subsidize that access (for example, through the FCC's universal service fund) to ensure that it becomes widespread. Politicians, scholars, and various advocates find themselves on all sides of this issue. In the opinion of the Progressive Policy Institute, an arm of the Democratic Leadership Council, the goal of the government should be to "provide sufficient free access to the Internet" so all individuals will have access to emerging technologies and realize the benefits of the developing network.[38] Others are not sure the government should be involved in providing access, noting that current rates of telephone penetration might have occurred even without government intervention.[39] Some strongly opposed to mandating universal access claim that such actions are "almost always antithetical to efficient pricing and ultimately to competition."[40]

On the more general question of whether firms should receive special treatment, through either subsidization or monopoly protection, in order to help them achieve critical mass, some say the government may find it worthwhile to sponsor "demonstration projects" to stimulate interest; however, "one should not underesti-

38. Atkinson, Court, and Ward (1999: 40).
39. See Shapiro and Varian (1997).
40. White (1999: 32).

mate the ingenuity of the private sector in dealing with network externalities." In other words, the private sector, more often than not, should be able to overcome the coordination problems associated with introducing new systems of products and establishing a market presence.[41] Illustrating this sentiment, studies of the evolution of the fax machine market suggest the point at which a market obtains critical mass is independent of market structure. Hence in the absence of any sort of external coordination by nonmarket forces, monopoly, oligopoly, or perfect competition can theoretically produce equally desirable outcomes with respect to technology diffusion.[42]

Summary and Implications

The sizable body of research on the general economic phenomena that can be classified as "network effects" may have a number of implications for the development of electronic markets and the Internet. Clearly, many topics relating to the bricks-and-mortar world—such as database access, communications systems, uniform standards—have electronic counterparts. At the same time, the rapid development of new technologies is posing a challenge to traditional concepts. In discussing these issues, one might wonder to what extent network effects actually exist and whether there is any empirical evidence to suggest certain market structures differ from others in their competitive effects.[43] If network effects are merely a theoretical concept, then it seems that government antitrust authorities should treat Internet-related markets like any other sort of product market or distribution channel in determining the presence (or lack) of viable competition.

41. Shapiro and Varian (1997: 17).
42. Economides and Himmelberg (1995).
43. See, for example, Liebowitz and Margolis (1994).

This concern speaks to the broader question of what, precisely, constitutes a network effect. Taken at the most basic definition, network effects may be considered a property of virtually any product, service, or system. But is such an expansive definition empirically accurate? The negative relationship between product price and network size is often cited as evidence of network effects, but such a relationship could emanate from any of several factors besides the presence of network effects, including something as basic as economies of scale with respect to the cost of inputs.[44] Unfortunately, when one focuses on such trends as price and production levels, it is impossible to distinguish between observationally equivalent phenomena, each of which would justify different methods of government intervention.[45]

There is, of course, ample empirical evidence of the presence of network effects in markets such as home computers, computer spreadsheet programs, and automated teller machines.[46] All the same, it may be very difficult to determine whether a given change in the relationship between price and market structure is a result of network effects or some underlying economies of scale particular to the market in question. These kinds of vagaries create many complex issues for antitrust authorities to consider.

In the United States, it is not illegal to exercise lawfully obtained market power. If a firm is exerting market power to obtain supracompetitive profits, then one must ask how it obtained and maintains that power. In most cases, one of the following factors will be

44. Liebowitz and Margolis (1994). For such a negative relationship to be observed, the "technological externalities" that follow from increased network size on the part of producers would likely lead to cost savings that exceed the increases in value to individual consumers from network growth (the latter would usually cause prices to increase, not decrease).

45. Liebowitz and Margolis (1994: 138).

46. Goolsbee and Klenow (1999); Gandal (1994); Saloner and Shepard (1995).

instrumental in achieving market power: some underlying economies of scale (that might lead to a natural monopoly), the production of a superior product, the existence of legal sanction (such as patents or licenses), the presence of network effects (such as "tipping"), or some form of anticompetitive practice (such as exclusion or predation). If the power was created through the last channel, then current antitrust policy should be able to address the problem. The same can be said for economies of scale (although outcomes that could follow from regulatory intervention may be arguably inefficient, economically speaking), superior product design, and, obviously, legal sanction.

In the event that market power is acquired because of the presence of network effects, however, it is unclear whether the government can, or should, intervene to regulate market activities. First, as noted earlier, it is difficult to determine whether network effects are indeed the source of market power; therefore authorities might be reluctant to intervene, for fear of taking inappropriate action. Second, even if market power could be shown to follow from network effects, it may be difficult to demonstrate that a firm came to dominate the market because of its conscious exploitation of existing network effects through some "attempt at monopolization."[47] To establish this latter condition, one would undoubtedly have to raise a host of other, fairly messy, questions. Should normal business trends such as price wars be deemed unfair conduct, if the price war led to industry tipping and subsequent monopoly? Can a firm be classified as having market power if there are negligible entry costs, but no firm will choose to enter because it stands no chance of achieving viable scale, given that the entrenched firm

47. As a matter of government enforcement policy, the Federal Trade Commission (1996, chap. 9) explores these issues in the context of competition policy in high-tech and developing marketplaces.

could profitably lower prices slightly and expand its network size even further?[48]

These questions are not trivial, and they will likely engage regulators in the coming years as the Internet expands to touch more industries and channels of commerce. A useful exercise for future research may be to theoretically (and empirically) distinguish between market power rooted in normal competitive responses and in anticompetitive exploitations of network effects. Such work can serve as a useful guide for government antitrust policy.

48. See Farrell and Saloner (1986).

CHAPTER SIX

TAXATION

Unlike most of the topics covered earlier in the discussion, the subject of this chapter is at the forefront of recent public policy debates: whether the government should impose new taxes upon Internet commerce. If so, which level of government should have taxing authority? How should a given taxation system be implemented? These questions have recently been raised by small businesses, local governments, online merchants, and a host of other interests. This chapter presents a brief review of the legal and legislative history surrounding the issue, indicates some of the research done on the matter, and demonstrates that the issue is neither clearcut nor likely to be resolved anytime in the near future.

Legal and Legislative History

The current debate over Internet taxation has many parallels in controversies over taxing mail-order catalog sales. In transaction formats alone, at least for physical goods, the two channels of commerce are virtually identical. Neither the Internet nor catalog sales require any sort of bricks-and-mortar outlet for commerce to proceed. In both cases, a consumer might in theory be ordering from a company that keeps its stock in a nondescript warehouse for the sole purpose of processing mail- or e-orders. Even more extreme is the possibility that a consumer might be ordering from a company that owns absolutely no capital or inventory but simply supplies orders on demand from producers to consumers. Given that consumers may be purchasing goods across state lines, questions have arisen about which body possesses the authority to (and should) collect taxes from such sales.

The question of whether remote sellers have an obligation to collect sales taxes from out-of-state buyers was addressed in two seminal Supreme Court cases: *National Bellas Hess* v. *Department of Revenue of the State of Illinois* (386 U.S. 753, 1967) and *Quill* v. *North Dakota* (504 U.S. 298, 1992). Their decisions established the current environment in which remote (that is, catalog) sales take place. Currently, companies cannot be compelled to collect sales taxes on those transactions that occur in a state where they do not have a "physical nexus," which is loosely defined as a geographical presence. The same standard has been conventionally adopted for electronic commerce as facilitated by the Internet.

Although companies cannot be compelled to collect taxes on Internet sales that occur outside of the state in which they possess a nexus, in most states individual consumers are still considered responsible for paying taxes. Specifically, in most taxing jurisdictions, consumers are subject to paying "use" taxes for goods that are bought outside of the jurisdiction in question. The use tax rate is typically the same level as the given jurisdiction's sales tax rate and is usually applied to the same kinds of goods covered by the sales tax. While such an institution might allow local governments to retain the tax base that is theoretically being lost to mail-order or Internet transactions, use taxes are somewhat ineffective, which should not be so surprising. Most consumers are completely unaware that their purchases are subject to such taxes; and even if they are aware, the rate of compliance is very low. If local governments are to hold on to such tax revenue, it seems necessary that they be allowed to collect taxes on Internet sales in some capacity.

Beginning in 1997, state and local governments, concerned that consumer migration to the web would drastically reduce their available tax base, began pressuring lawmakers to introduce Internet tax legislation. Their cause was strengthened by the interests of small businesses that were beginning to feel the competitive pressure of online stores, which were able to offer lower prices, at least partly because of a tax advantage. Not willing to wait for national legislation, state legislatures considered passing new legislation specifically for electronic commerce, which would allow them to tax remote sales. Most state legislatures were not considering legislation that would make it legal to tax electronic commerce per se, but rather legislation that would require online merchants to collect existing use taxes owed by those customers who lived in a state in which the firm did not have a physical presence.

Recognizing the momentum behind the issue, and realizing the speed with which trends on the Internet can change, Representative Christopher Cox (R-Calif.) and Senator Ron Wyden (D-Oreg.) introduced the Internet Tax Freedom Act (ITFA) in 1998 to address the issue. Passed as part of the Omnibus Appropriations Act of 1998, the ITFA placed a three-year moratorium on new Internet taxes and created the Advisory Commission on Electronic Commerce to study issues related to the taxation of the Internet. The commission was to consist of nineteen members appointed by Congress and representing business, the federal government, and state and local governments. Its term was to expire in April 2000, at which point it was to present its recommendations to Congress about the appropriate course of action for future Internet tax policy.

The commission held its first meeting in June 1999, in

Williamsburg, Virginia, and among the attendees was Federal Trade Commissioner Orson Swindle, who, in his speech, pointed to the many complicated issues that the body would need to address. As Commissioner Swindle noted, "with approximately 30,000 taxing jurisdictions, compliance becomes a significant obstacle. The Internet is inherently susceptible to multiple and discriminatory taxation in a way that commerce conducted in more traditional ways is not."[1] In view of these and other concerns, the commissioner stated, coming up with a clear method of defining the Internet tax structure would be "very tricky."

In the months following the first meeting, the advisory commission considered various options, ranging from no tax to a flat tax for all electronic commerce. Despite the fact that the ITFA mandated a three-year moratorium, members of Congress, as well as representatives from local governments, began pushing different legislative proposals for dealing with the taxation issue. Wyden and Cox, original cosponsors of the ITFA, introduced legislation asking the Word Trade Organization to enact a permanent global moratorium on taxation of Internet commerce. Similarly, Senator John McCain (R-Ariz.) introduced a bill that would have permanently extended the ITFA moratorium after its expiration in 2001. On the other side, arguing that local governments stood to lose $11 billion a year, organizations such as the U.S. Conference of Mayors organized panels to lobby Congress for taxation power.[2] Representing this school of thought, Senator Ernest Hollings (D-S.C.) introduced a bill calling for a uniform 5 percent tax on all remote sales, including Internet and conventional mail-order transactions. In early December 1999, the Clinton administration openly criticized a plan

1. Swindle (1999).
2. Cottman (1999).

proposed by Governor James R. Gilmore III (R-Va.), chairman of the Commission on Electronic Commerce, that would have made all online purchases exempt from sales taxes, arguing that such a policy would put offline firms at a disadvantage and deprive local governments of potential revenues.[3]

As January 2000 dawned, it was unclear what direction the debate would take, and there was little sign of consensus in the air. The tax question became an election issue when Senator McCain proposed a permanent moratorium on Internet sales taxes during his bid for the Republican presidential nomination in the spring primaries. In March 2000, in its final official meeting, the Advisory Commission on Electronic Commerce found itself unable to put forward any official recommendations to Congress because a required supermajority of thirteen members could not agree on any tax-related proposal. One of the main reasons a supermajority was not secured was that the administration representatives and committee members from state and local governments abstained on necessary votes. Governor Gilmore criticized these abstentions, but the administration representatives responded that the commission had not been operating with the general consensus of the relevant shareholders.[4]

Although the commission was unable to develop "official" recommendations, congressional leaders urged its members to issue a report on those proposals that had secured a simple majority. The final report recommended, among other things, a five-year extension on the existing ban on new Internet taxes. This recommendation was quickly incorporated into a bill in the House of Representatives (coincidentally, sponsored by Representatives Cox and

3. Chandrasekaran (1999b).
4. Schwartz (2000a).

Wyden) and sailed through the House in late May by a final vote of 352 to 75. While the bill's passage was hailed as a victory by the private sector and the Republican leadership, not every industry leader enthusiastically approved. In a June 2000 hearing ("Removing Barriers to the New Economy") before the Joint Economic Committee, Intel Chairman Andrew Grove took a surprising stand when he argued in favor of Internet sales taxes, saying that he did not see any "justification" for the tax exemption.[5] Independent of Grove's concerns, as the bill wound its way through the Senate (and through this entire process more generally), several economic arguments and justifications (discussed in the next section) were being voiced to support the relevant camps.[6]

Current Research on Internet Taxation

The current debate has placed the onus on scholars to establish why electronic commerce should, or should not, be taxed. In response, a few are addressing the equity issues associated with taxing electronic commerce, mainly in theoretical terms, supported by arguments from traditional public finance economics. Charles McLure, who compares e-commerce events to the history of mail-order catalogs, states that electronic commerce should be taxed.[7] Responding to the conventional "infant industry" arguments that might support a moratorium on Internet taxation until the electronic commerce channels are more "mature," McLure claims that such policies inevitably keep favored industries from ever "growing up." Furthermore, he argues, substantial horizontal and vertical equity issues

5. Schwartz (2000b).

6. For a succinct history of the legal and legislative issues surrounding Internet taxation, see Lukas (1999).

7. McLure (1999).

are at stake: not taxing the Internet is, in effect, providing an indirect transfer of wealth to the rich (many of whom engage in electronic commerce, more so than the poor). If the Internet is not
subject to taxation, McLure adds, economic decisions will suffer
"gross inequities and distortions" and "local merchants [will] face
unfair competition from out-of-state vendors who pay no sales tax."[8]

The question of whether electronic commerce must be taxed
to level the playing field between the Internet and bricks-and-
mortar outlets has been addressed in several studies, but with mixed
results.[9] Those who favor taxation argue that exemptions for electronic commerce, combined with the current taxation system, will
lead to significant distortions that will put conventional retailers
at a great disadvantage. Others claim that the tax differential will
merely inspire conventional retailers to migrate to the Internet,
and that if state governments are genuinely concerned about equity, they should consider "harmonizing tax rates downward for
local retailers," rather than imposing new taxes on the Internet to
eliminate the tax differences.[10]

Some empirical work has been done on the possible effects of
imposing sales taxes and compliance costs on the Internet. To this
end, Austan Goolsbee has attempted to determine the price elasticity of demand associated with Internet sales and the sales and consumption choices that would follow from such a tax.[11] Drawing upon
data from a private survey conducted by Forrester Research in late
1997, he examined the purchasing decisions of 25,000 users as a
function of their demographic traits and their residential charac-

8. McLure (1998b: 11).
9. See, for example, Lukas (1999); McLure (1998a).
10. Lukas (1999: 16).
11. Goolsbee (2000).

teristics, including local sales taxation rate. His primary objectives were to determine how the local sales tax rate affected an individual's choice to purchase something online and how it affected the average amount of money spent online by the typical consumer.

Goolsbee first analyzed what drives a shopper to commit to purchasing something on the web. Controlling for a variety of conventional demographic characteristics such as income, education, and age, he found that the probability of buying something online grows as the local sales tax rate increases. Furthermore, this finding is robust to a variety of specifications, controlling for such features as consumer technological savviness, and general computer access. To determine how offline sales taxes affect the levels of consumers' online expenditures, Goolsbee analyzed individual spending patterns as a function of the local sales tax rate, as well as the usual demographic variables and others aimed at controlling for technological sophistication. Here, Goolsbee found that the coefficient on local tax rate is positive and significant, which implies that the higher the local sales tax rate, the greater the amount of money the average consumer spends online. Applying existing tax rates to the Internet, Goolsbee concluded, will reduce the number of buyers online from 20 percent to 25 percent and reduce total sales by 25 percent to 30 percent.

Three aspects of these findings led Goolsbee to argue against instituting a tax for electronic commerce. First, the elasticity of demand for conventional mail-order sales indicates that mail-order and Internet sales seem equally responsive to taxation.[12] Hence, if taxes are raised on the Internet, consumers are likely to migrate to conventional mail-order sales and no sizable revenues will be raised.

---

12. Goolsbee analyzes the propensity of consumers to buy personal computers online, through direct mail, or in stores as a function of local tax rates.

Second, enforcement would be mired in complications, both in identifying what is actually taxable, and in devising actual collection
methods. At the same time, low/nonexistent tax rates might have
positive externalities, in that they would encourage more consumers to experiment with and gain confidence in the medium. This
would yield a larger potential tax base should the government choose
to tax e-commerce in the future.[13]

Some might question the robustness of Goolsbee's findings, however, given the growth of the web. Internet commerce has exploded
since the data were collected in 1997, and it is conceivable that
Goolsbee's study suffers from a selection bias in that a majority of
the consumers in the sample were more technologically sophisticated and more tax-sensitive than the typical offline consumer. To
address this question, Goolsbee revisited the 1997 database, in conjunction with a survey from the following year (also conducted by
Forrester Research).[14] He investigated whether his earlier results
would be robust if the sample was more representative of the average consumer. When Goolsbee looked at the entire sample of users,
he again found the coefficient on local tax rates to be significant
and positive. But when he partitioned the sample into two groups—
experienced and new users (defined as those who have been connected to the Internet for at least two years)—the tax sensitivities
were not very large (or even significant) for new users.

Goolsbee next asked whether this difference in tax sensitivity
between "generations" follows from user heterogeneity or educa-

13. Along these lines, the use of low taxation to facilitate Internet proliferation is somewhat analogous to the results obtained by Rohlfs (1974) and Cabral,
Salant, and Woroch (1997) regarding penetration pricing in the presence of
network externalities. The veracity of this claim is obviously an empirical matter that should be studied further.
14. Goolsbee (1999).

tion about the tax code. In other words, are new users simply not as sensitive to tax rates as old users, or are they simply not aware of the relevant differences in tax policies between the Internet and bricks-and-mortar outlets, and thus merely appear to be less sensitive than experienced surfers? The policy implication from such a distinction, as noted by Goolsbee, is obvious: if these new users flooding the web are relatively insensitive to sales taxes, then arguments against taxation because of high consumer elasticities are moot. If, on the other hand, these new users are simply ignorant about the tax system, and upon learning the system they become tax-sensitive, then his earlier results might still be relevant, and implementing taxes on electronic commerce will likely have large chilling effects on electronic commerce. When Goolsbee controls for demographic similarities across generations, his results suggest that consumers become more aware of the tax code as they become more experienced with the Internet and hence become more sensitive to local sales taxes in their purchase decisions. Therefore, there seems to be a pervasive (and sizable) tax sensitivity on the part of consumers that would negatively affect online commerce, were sales taxes to be instituted.

Another question that states will want to consider is how much revenue do they stand to lose here? As noted earlier, state governments tend to think that they could lose billions of dollars in tax revenue if e-commerce goes untaxed. One figure recently cited by the National Governors' Association (NGA) puts the potential revenue loss following from Internet and mail-order sales at $20 billion a year by 2002.[15] If such figures are accurate, then it is hardly surprising that local governments are pressing the case for taxation so aggressively; with such large quantities of funds at stake, local infra-

15. Associated Press (1998).

structure might be impaired if appropriate legislation is not implemented. The important word in the preceding sentence, however, is "if." States and local municipalities base much of their argument on the notion that the Internet is indeed taking such a sizable portion of their revenues out of their grasp.

To test the validity of this claim, Goolsbee and Jonathan Zittrain investigate where states' revenues are currently coming from and how the Internet is likely to affect them.[16] Contrary to popular belief, the authors conclude, the Internet will not wreak financial havoc on local finances in the foreseeable future, and tax legislation is neither a necessary nor an appropriate manner with which to address the concerns of government agencies. The figure cited by the NGA, the authors point out, is inappropriate for three main reasons. First, it includes business-to-business commerce, which is currently exempt from sales tax regardless of the method of transaction. Second, the estimate ignores the possibility that trade created through the Internet might be generating much of the commerce observed. In other words, these potential revenues would not even exist in the first place if it were not for the Internet, and thus it is inappropriate to view them as "lost" revenues. Third, even if the NGA is identifying valid taxable items, their treatment of such items artificially inflates the potential loss. For example, the NGA counts the online sale of home computers as a revenue loss even though most online computer sellers collect/pay sales taxes in some capacity.

After stripping away those categories of goods that are either already being taxed or not subject to sales taxes, Goolsbee and Zittrain claim that only $2.5 billion of sales are subject to taxes that are not being collected, which is equivalent to a tax revenue loss of $210

16. Goolsbee and Zittrain (1999).

million to $430 million in 1998.[17] Contingent on a high rate of growth
in electronic commerce, projected tax losses will come to about $2.5
billion in 2002 and $3.5 billion in 2003, which is less than 2 percent
of potential sales tax revenue, a far smaller figure than that being
cited by the NGA. Conventional arguments about the need for taxes
to "level the playing field" or ameliorate distributional concerns are
unfounded, the authors say, and push for a moratorium on Internet
taxes so that usage might proliferate across all demographic groups
and the maximum benefits of the network might be realized.

Robert Cline and Thomas Neubig perform a similar revenue de-
composition exercise on sales data from 1998 to determine how
much governments plausibly stand to lose to the Internet, absent
new taxation legislation.[18] After discarding those categories of goods
that cannot be considered revenue losers, Cline and Neubig determine that the total amount of untaxed sales in 1998 was approximately $2.6 billion, a figure very close to that determined by Goolsbee
and Zittrain. From this estimate, they calculate that the actual revenue loss to the Internet in 1998 was only $170 million. Given that
current tax losses amount to only about 0.1 percent of total revenues, the notion of a tax "crisis" is inappropriate, they argue, and
state and federal governments have plenty of time in which to develop an efficient and useful taxation scheme (if any) for electronic
commerce.

According to the calculations of Donald Bruce and William Fox,
however, future state revenue losses from electronic commerce are

17. This $2.5 billion figure can only be accepted, the authors note, if one
assumes that somehow taxes would be collected on all auction transactions as if
they were sales made through classified ads. The estimated size of the total tax
loss is subject to variations in predicted growth in electronic commerce by the
end of 1998.
18. Cline and Neubig (1999b).

far higher. Because of increases in remote sales (through catalog and cross-state shopping), shifts in consumption patterns toward tax-exempt services, and the expansion of legislated tax-exemptions for certain products, states were already experiencing a consistent decline in their sales tax bases before the advent of electronic commerce. Bruce and Fox thus examine the extent to which the growth of electronic commerce might effectively speed up this downward slide in state tax revenues. Using conventional financial forecasting techniques, they estimate that state and local losses in sales tax revenue and general narrowing of the tax base will amount to $23.8 billion in 2003. Of that figure, $10.8 billion can be classified as "incremental" revenue losses due to electronic commerce, meaning those transactions for which taxes would have been collected in the absence of electronic commerce. At the individual state level, incremental losses due to e-commerce push state revenues down by anywhere from 0.90 percent in Massachusetts to 2.62 percent in Texas. To compensate for these losses while maintaining constant government revenues, states would have to raise their sales tax rates from 0.45 percent in Wyoming to 0.91 percent in Washington. To Bruce and Fox, these findings suggest that electronic commerce has in fact "accelerated" the already existing downward trend in state and local tax bases. Furthermore, this increased burden might induce local governments to either change their fiscal structure to derive their revenues from alternative sources (such as property or income taxes) or reduce their overall expenditures altogether such that they are less dependent on the shrinking tax funds.

Although these figures seem out of line with those of the other two studies—$10.8 billion is certainly much higher than the $3.5 billion estimated by Goolsbee and Zittrain—the $10.8 billion still amounts to only 1.52 percent of what Bruce and Fox estimate to be total state tax revenue for 2003. Hence, it is not obvious that this forecasted tax loss is leading to a substantial revenue crisis on the part of the states. Remember, too, that the forecasts in each of these studies follow from a particular set of assumptions about current and future economic conditions. Different assumptions can lead to wildly different findings. For many of the assumptions made by Bruce and Fox, "empirical guidance is either limited or nonexistent."[19] While this does not necessarily rule out the validity of any of the findings just discussed, it places an additional burden on the reader to evaluate which set of assumptions is more plausible in order to assess which results are more likely.

Another factor to consider in assessing tax loss is the possible compliance costs associated with different tax policies. Sales taxes of various forms are currently imposed by forty-six states and almost 7,500 local governments in the United States. These taxes are not typically uniform across all goods, but rather applied to certain distinct commodities, depending upon the jurisdiction in question. Absent some sort of technological intervention, requiring online merchants to determine what is taxable and the appropriate rate for a given destination as well as ensuring collection might place significant burdens on retailers. (This is the implicit rationale behind the court decisions in the landmark mail-order cases.) Although it is difficult to calculate the relative compliance costs involved with any accuracy, a recent study from Washington State offers some insight into the kind of burden the collection of all taxes on all online sales might impose.[20]

In fulfilling the statutory requirements of the 1998 Washington State supplemental budget law, the Washington State Department of Revenue distributed a survey to 3,400 retailers in Washington

19. Bruce and Fox (2000: fn. 21).
20. Washington State Department of Revenue (1998).

and Oregon to determine the costs incurred by retailers in complying with collecting and remitting state and local sales taxes. The response rate was 51 percent for Washington retailers and 36 percent for Oregon retailers. Responses indicated that the total cost to retailers for collecting and remitting sales taxes is 4.23 percent of total state and local taxes collected. But the burdens associated with tax collection and processing are not uniform across all sizes of business: they range from 0.97 percent for large retailers to 6.47 percent to small retailers. In order to collect and remit sales taxes in their own state, small retailers are spending about $6.50 of every $100 collected on determining the relevant tax rates and exemptions for the goods being sold. It seems reasonable to suppose that these costs would be higher if merchants were required to collect taxes from states in which they do not have a presence and intimate knowledge of the tax code.[21]

Summary and Implications

There seem to be two schools of thought on Internet taxation. One favors mandating new sales taxes for the web or mandatory collection of existing taxes, in part to make up for the lost revenues to state and local governments that will likely occur without such taxes. For some, the desire to maintain an economically neutral sales tax system also weighs heavily for the adoption of Internet taxes. The other group is opposed to Internet taxes, first because the relevant levels of revenue at stake are not particularly large. Implementing taxes on the web, they argue, will only serve to chill online pur-

21. Cline and Neubig (1999a) provide a succinct discussion of the findings of the Washington State Department of Revenue study as well as a brief picture of the complexities that surround the sales tax code in various municipalities across the country.

chases and electronic commerce more generally. Also retailers will probably be burdened with large costs arising from collecting and remitting such taxes. Although this latter problem may be resolved though technological or other means, no obvious solution is currently available.

The body of work on Internet taxation, though moderate in size, provides a first-order approximation of the relative effects associated with mandating taxes on Internet sales. As electronic commerce continues to grow, several issues will need closer attention to determine appropriate tax policy. Chief among these are (obviously) the feasible magnitude of the revenues forgone by local governments absent Internet taxes versus the cost of tax collection, as well as the likely effects of taxes on purchases. Conventional public finance scholarship has clearly shown that differential sales tax rates can lead to the migration of commercial transactions toward jurisdictions that most favor consumers.[22] While the studies discussed earlier in the chapter would seem to support this conclusion, further analysis would confirm whether these findings are robust or merely the symptoms of preliminary shocks being experienced by an "infant" industry.

Attention should also be given to the actual harm bricks-and-mortar businesses will experience in competing with outlets whose goods are not subject to sales tax. As already noted, theory would argue that taxing identical goods at different rates would likely lead consumers to shift their purchases toward the lower-taxing outlets. Such a shift might coincide with a pro-competitive outcome if the less-expensive outlets are able to provide lower prices owing to economies of scale, but if the price differential is solely a function of the

22. See Mikesell (1970); Walsh and Jones (1988).

lack of sales tax, then such consumption shifts are inefficient.[23] Ideally, one would need to have access to panel data on consumers' retail buying habits in both bricks-and-mortar outlets and online over time to see if consumers are shifting their purchases as hypothesized.[24] Unfortunately, no such data currently exist. Future research might profit from collecting such data to examine whether the theoretical inefficiencies that follow from differential tax rates are being empirically realized on the Internet.

Another important question to consider is what strategies brick-and-mortar firms might employ to retain customers and reduce the ability of online firms to free-ride on them with respect to product display, showroom expertise, and the like. The ease with which customers can wander around a real-world store examining products and then purchase them online, usually for a lower price (and to avoid taxes) obviously compromises the profitability of maintaining a showroom. Would there be an inefficient reduction in offline stores as a result? What measures could brick-and-mortar stores take to keep the dollars in their shops?

Legislation—perhaps mandating a uniform tax on all Internet sales—or technology will probably help keep compliance costs from becoming cumbersome. Several software companies are already developing innovative programs that will allow retailers to instantly calculate the relevant sales taxes for purchases made in remote locations. While the costs of these packages may still be too high for widespread use among small retailers, they will probably come down

23. In addressing the subject of tax evasion, Trandel (1992) argues that differential tax rates, while possibly welfare-reducing with respect to aggregate state revenues and consumer purchase decisions, might also enhance welfare, in that the tax evasion that follows might serve to drive product prices toward marginal costs. Hence the overall efficiency effects of differential tax rates and potential evasion seem ambiguous.

24. Goolsbee and Zittrain (1999).

in response to the increased demand that would come with mandated taxes.[25]

One idea proposed to the Advisory Commission on Electronic Commerce would be to transfer taxes directly from consumers to governments, using the credit card companies as an intermediary.[26] Taking the collection and remittance responsibilities out of retailers' hands would, in theory, greatly ease the complications associated with applying sales taxes to online commerce. As of early 2000, several companies had announced their intention to release sales-tax accounting software packages that could calculate sales taxes across 60,000 potential tax jurisdictions.[27] One way or another, compliance costs seem destined to fall to levels that might facilitate the implementation of taxation schemes.

Yet another possibility would be to completely restructure tax laws so as to significantly change sales taxes or do away with them altogether. Policymakers have at least four options here, says Hal Varian: maintain the status quo, completely ban Internet taxation, mandate out-of-state vendors to collect local use taxes (through either congressional statute or state initiatives), or eliminate state and local sales taxes altogether in favor of a revenue-equivalent increase in income tax or the establishment of a consumption tax.[28] Such taxes, Varian says, would be less distortionary and less cumbersome to implement than existing sales taxes. He also encourages the federal government to stay out of the debate and leave it to the states to decide what taxation scheme is appropriate. In addition, he encourages scholars to try to determine specific methods by which to implement revenue-equivalent alternatives to sales taxes.

25. Lukas (1999) quotes a price of $20,000.
26. Chartrand (1999).
27. Jones (2000).
28. Varian (2000, 1999a).

Although the idea of abolishing sales taxes might seem implausible, recent political developments lend credibility to the argument. In February 2000, two bills were introduced into the Virginia legislature aimed at abolishing the state's 4.5 percent sales tax. Those in favor of the legislation felt that it was an appropriate way to level the playing field between traditional merchants and online firms. The lost revenues from sales tax, they argued, would be more than recouped from the boom in the state's income tax revenue.[29] Whether any state will implement such legislation, only time will tell.

From a strictly economic standpoint, it is very difficult to argue in favor of a tax advantage for online firms. As recent developments with the Advisory Commission on Electronic Commerce indicate, however, a host of practical and political problems stand in the way of developing a suitable policy recommendation. The final solution will no doubt revolve around several of the issues discussed here: consumers' responses to tax differentials, the potential effects of "forgone revenues" on local communities, and the threats to "main-street businesses" and bricks-and-mortar outlets posed by e-commerce. But each of these matters is politically charged and will likely keep Capitol Hill and state governments fully occupied over the next few years.

29. Timberg (2000).

CHAPTER SEVEN

CONCLUSION

NO ONE CAN deny that the Internet has had a noticeable effect on society in general and popular perceptions of the economy in particular. Originally developed as a tool for academia and government, the Internet is now accessible to (and incorporated into the daily lives of) people from virtually all demographic groups. Faced with the possibilities of quick wealth in electronic commerce, entrepreneurs have begun experimenting with hugely diverse business models, ranging from conventional sales transactions to unorthodox practices such as providing free content and products in the hopes of securing a sizable market share. Though many remain skeptical about the viability of certain business practices or uncertain about the likely evolution of the Internet, most would agree that substantial change will occur in the future.

This book has presented some of the relevant economic research surrounding the Internet with a view to suggesting what the future might plausibly bring. But there is still much to learn about this new transactions medium, especially through theoretical and large-sample empirical research. The possible paths of investigation are numerous and will only multiply as more data become available and new methodologies are developed. The following paragraphs offer a smattering of these possibilities.

The subject of access provision, for instance, might be explored through simulations or experimental settings to determine which of the various access pricing models perform better from a social efficiency standpoint, under different assumptions about consumers' demands, accounting costs, and other administrative concerns. In addition, it would be important to accurately identify consumers' willingness to pay for usage-sensitive pricing mechanisms and to devise appropriate accounting tools to implement such models. As the electronic marketplace matures, it will also be possible to answer more questions about electronic commerce: about the magnitude and significance of differences between online and offline prices, the potential for online collusion, and the effectiveness of the Internet and electronic markets as a clearinghouse for second-hand goods. These and other such investigations will shed much light on the Internet's potential for "frictionless commerce."

Questions about government antitrust policy might become clearer, too, through a continuation of work already begun on the distinctions between market power that arises from normal competitive responses and market power that arises from anticompetitive exploitation of network externalities. Current findings about consumers' online purchasing patterns, compliance costs, and revenue streams for local governments could also be used as a springboard for deeper explorations of internet taxation. Here it would be important to establish whether such factors are indicative of a long-run stable outcome or reflect a shock to the system associated with an "infant industry." As discussions of tax system reform evolve, it also would be useful to understand the degree to which alternative taxation schemes might be revenue-equivalent to, yet less distortionary than, conventional sales taxes.

Beyond these topics, several subjects not addressed in this book will become equally important to public policy in the future and deserve close study. In May 2000 attention was drawn to a case involving the start-up "Napster," based in San Mateo, California, in which music recordings were being digitally downloaded from the web (via Napster) without the consent of the artists.[1] This possible facilitation of copyright infringement has rekindled serious questions about how the Internet will affect conventional notions of intellectual property.

Another contentious issue reemerged in full force in May 2000 when the Federal Trade Commission delivered its report on online privacy to Congress. Arguing that industry had made insufficient progress in self-regulation, the FTC recommended that Congress pass legislation requiring all websites to abide by the four "Fair Information Privacy Principles."[2] Specifically, firms would have to (1) give consumers notice about what information is being collected about them, (2) allow them to choose whether or not to provide such information, (3) provide them with reasonable access to the information a website has about them so that they can verify its accuracy and alter it if necessary, and (4) guarantee the security of the data collected from them. Because the Clinton administration and congressional majorities disagreed with the views of the FTC, it is difficult to predict what direction the debate will take.[3] That is particularly why further scholarship about the economics of personal privacy and information sharing is vital. Along with work on the costs of implementing regulatory mechanisms, it will serve to increase our understanding of this controversial topic and help guide policymakers in the future.

Chapter 4 of this book, on electronic commerce, drew attention to business-to-consumer (B2C) transactions but only touched on

1. Hartigan (2000).
2. Federal Trade Commission (2000).
3. Labaton (2000).

another important section of Internet-based commerce: the fast-growing business-to-business (B2B) transactions. Recognizing the web's potential for streamlining inventory processes, several companies are offering their wares online to firms that engage in either production processes or commercial retail. At the same time, new industrial alliances have emerged as numerous B2B exchanges have been established in the hope of reducing production costs and offering consumers more customized products.

A clear example of such a case is the February 2000 announcement by General Motors, Ford, and DaimlerChrysler that they want to establish a joint Internet auction site with which to acquire their production materials.[4] Although auto executives have predicted that this will cut production costs by up to 10 percent, concern about the potential for collusion (combined with the monstrous size of the endeavor) motivated the Federal Trade Commission to review the merger plans.[5] With the potential to generate $2.7 billion in trade by 2004, there is a significant incentive to evaluate the prospects for anticompetitive outcomes as well as to develop methods and tools for facilitating B2B.[6]

These are only a few of the multitude of issues that continue to surface as the web and Internet usage expand and become relevant to more sectors of our economy and society. This book will, I hope, serve as a useful roadmap of relevant research pertaining to some economic aspects of the Internet and provide a solid starting point from which to begin future inquiry. As we look at the world quickly evolving around us, there is no doubt that we are living in interesting times. The question is, where will we go next?

4. Bradsher (2000).
5. Rowley (2000).
6. Forrester Research (2000).

REFERENCES

Abbate, Janet. 1999. *Inventing the Internet.* Cambridge, Mass.: MIT Press.

Adar, Eytan, and Bernardo A. Huberman. 1999. "The Economics of Surfing." Typescript, Xerox Palo Alto Research Center.

Akerlof, G. 1970. "The Market for 'Lemons': Quality Uncertainty and the Market Mechanism." *Quarterly Journal of Economics* 84 (3): 488–500.

Anania, Loretta, and Richard Jay Solomon. 1997. "Flat—The Minimalist Price." In *Internet Economics,* edited by Lee W. McKnight and Joseph P. Bailey. Cambridge, Mass.: MIT Press.

Areeda, Philip, and Donald F. Turner. 1975. "Predatory Pricing and Related Practices under Section 2 of the Sherman Act." *Harvard Law Review* 88 (February): 697–733.

Associated Press. 1998. "Governors Fear Tax Loss from Internet; States' Surpluses Treated Cautiously." *Boston Globe,* December 31.

Atkinson, Robert D., and Randolph H. Court. 1998. *The New Economy Index: Understanding America's Economic Transformation.* Washington, D.C.: Progressive Policy Institute.

Atkinson, Robert D., Randolph H. Court, and Joseph M. Ward. 1999. *The State New Economy Index.* Washington, D.C.: Progressive Policy Institute.

Ausubel, Lawrence M., and Peter Cramton. 1998. "Demand Reduction and Inefficiency in Multi-Unit Auctions." Typescript, University of Maryland.

Axell, B. 1977. "Search Market Equilibrium." *Scandinavian Journal of Economics* 79 (1): 20–40.

Bailey, Joseph P. 1997. "The Economics of Internet Interconnection Agreements." In *Internet Economics,* edited by Lee W. McKnight and Joseph P. Bailey. Cambridge, Mass.: MIT Press.

―――. 1998a. "Electronic Commerce: Prices and Consumer Issues for Three Products: Books, Compact Discs, and Software." OCDE/GD(98)4. Organization for Economic Cooperation and Development, Paris.

―――. 1998b. "Intermediation and Electronic Markets: Aggregation and Pricing in Internet Commerce." Ph.D. diss., Technology, Management and Policy, Massachusetts Institute of Technology, Cambridge, Mass.

―――. 1998c. "Internet Price Discrimination: Self-Regulation, Public Policy, and Global Economic Commerce." Paper submitted to the 26th Annual Telecommunications Policy Research Conference Student Paper Competition, May 1.

Bailey, Joseph P., and Yannis Bakos. 1997. "An Exploratory Study of the Emerging Role of Electronic Intermediaries." *International Journal of Electronic Commerce,* 1 (3): 7–20.

Bakos, J. Yannis, 1997. "Reducing Buyer Search Costs: Implications for Electronic Marketplaces." *Management Science* 43 (12): 1676–92.

―――. 1998. "The Emerging Role of Electronic Marketplaces on the Internet." *Communications of the ACM* 41 (August): 35–42.

Bakos, J. Yannis, and Erik Brynjolfsson. 1999a. "Aggregation and Disaggregation of Information Goods: Implications for Bundling, Site Licensing, and Micropayment." In *Internet Publishing and Beyond: The Economics of Digital Information and Intellectual Property,* edited by Deborah Hurley, Brian Kahin, and Hal R. Varian. Cambridge, Mass.: MIT Press.

―――. 1999b. "Bundling and Competition on the Internet." Typescript, MIT Sloan School of Management.

―――. 1999c. "Bundling Information Goods: Pricing, Profits and Efficiency." *Management Science* 45 (12): 1613–30.

Balto, David. 1999. "Network Exclusivity: Antitrust Analysis to Promote Network Competition." *George Mason Law Review* 7 (3): 523–76.

Barua, Anitesh, Jon Pinnell, Jay Shutter, and Andrew B. Whinston. 1999. "Measuring the Internet Economy: An Exploratory Study." Typescript, University of Texas at Austin, Graduate School of Business.

Besen, Stanley M., and Joseph Farrell. 1994. "Choosing How to Compete: Strategies and Tactics in Standardization." *Journal of Economic Perspectives* 8 (2): 117–31.

Biglaiser, Gary. 1993. "Middlemen as Experts." *RAND Journal of Economics* 24 (2): 212–23.

Braden, Robert, David D. Clark, and Scott Shenker. 1994. "Integrated Services in the Internet Architecture: An Overview." Request for Comments 1663. Information Sciences Institute, University of Southern California, July.

Bradsher, Keith. 2000. "Carmakers to Buy Parts on Internet." *New York Times,* February 26.

Brownlee, Nevil. 1996. "Internet Pricing in Practice." In *Internet Economics,* edited by Lee W. McKnight and Joseph P. Bailey. Cambridge, Mass.: MIT Press.

Bruce, Donald, and William F. Fox. 2000. "E-Commerce in the Context of Declining State Sales Tax Bases." Typescript, University of Tennessee, Center for Business and Economic Research.

Brynjolfsson, Erik, and Michael D. Smith. 1999. "Frictionless Commerce? A Comparison of Internet and Conventional Retailers." Typescript, MIT Sloan School of Management.

Bulow, Jeremy. 1982. "Durable-Goods Monopolists." *Journal of Political Economy* 90 (2): 314–32.

Burgess, John. 1999. "Amazon Reverses on Hitler Book." *Washington Post,* November 18.

Cabral, Luis M. B., David J. Salant, and Glen A. Woroch. 1997. "Monopoly Pricing with Network Externalities." Typescript, University of California, Berkeley.

Calfee, John, and Clifford Winston. 1998. "The Value of Automobile Traffic Time: Implications for Congestion Policy." *Journal of Public Economics* 69 (1): 83–102.

Carmel, Erran, J. Eisenach, and T. Lenard. 1999. *Digital Economy Fact Book.* Washington, D.C.: Progress and Freedom Foundation.

Casey, Michael. 1999. "Power of the Internet Ensures Supply and Demand Will Never Be the Same." *Wall Street Journal,* October 18.

Chandrasekaran, Rajiv. 1999a. "Microsoft Ends Message War." *Washington Post,* November 19.

———. 1999b. "E-Commerce Tax Plan Assailed." *Washington Post,* December 11.

Chartrand, Sabra. 1999. "Collecting Sales Tax from the Internet." *Washington Post,* October 4.

Chiang, Raymond, and Chester S. Spatt. 1982. "Imperfect Price Discrimination and Welfare." *Review of Economic Studies* 49 (2): 153–81.

Choi, Soon-Young, Dale Stahl, and Andrew Whinston. 1997. *The Economics of Electronic Commerce.* Indianapolis, Ind.: Macmillan Technical.

Clark, David D. 1997. "Internet Cost Allocation and Pricing." In *Internet Economics,* edited by Lee W. McKnight and Joseph P. Bailey. Cambridge, Mass.: MIT Press.

Clark, David D., Scott Shenker, and Lixia Zhang. 1992. "Supporting Real-Time Applications in an Integrated Services Packet Network: Architecture and Mechanism." *Proceedings of SIGCOMM* 92: 14–16.

Clemons, Eric K., Il-Horn Hann, and Lorin M. Hitt. 1999. "The Nature of Competition in Electronic Markets: An Empirical Investigation of Online Travel Agent Offerings." Typescript, Wharton School, University of Pennsylvania.

Cline, Robert J., and Thomas S. Neubig. 1999a. "Masters of Complexity and Bearers of Great Burden: The Sales Tax System and Compliance Costs for Multistate Retailers." Technical Report, Ernst and Young Economics Consulting and Quantitative Analysis.

———. 1999b. "The Sky Is Not Falling: Why State and Local Revenues Were Not Significantly Impacted by the Internet in 1998." Technical Report, Ernst and Young Economics Consulting and Quantitative Analysis.

Coase, Ronald H. 1972. "Durability and Monopoly." *Journal of Law and Economics* 15 (April): 143–49.

Cocchi, Ron, Scott Shenker, Deborah Estrin, and Lixia Zhang. 1993. "Pricing in Computer Networks: Motivation, Formulation and Example." *IEE/ACM Transactions on Networking* 1 (6): 614–27.

Corts, Kenneth S. 1996. "On the Competitive Effects of Price-Matching Policies." *International Journal of Industrial Organization* 15: 283–99.

Cottman, Michael H. 1999. "Williams to Head Internet Panel." *Washington Post*, September 26.

Deneckere, Raymond J., and R. Preston McAfee. 1996. "Damaged Goods." *Journal of Economics and Management Strategy* 5 (2): 149–74.

Diamond, Peter A. 1971. "A Model of Price Adjustment." *Journal of Economic Theory* 3 (2) : 156–68.

Drezen, Richard. 2000. "A Dot-Com World." *Washington Post*, May 17.

Eaton, Johnathan, and Gene M. Grossman. 1986. "The Provision of Information as Marketing Strategy." *Oxford Economic Papers* 38 (3): 166–83.

Economides, Nicholas. 1996. "The Economics of Networks." *International Journal of Industrial Organization* 14 (2): 673–99.

Economides, Nicholas, and Charles Himmelberg. 1995. "Critical Mass and Network Evolution in Telecommunications." In *Toward a Competitive Telecommunications Industry: Selected Papers from the 1994 Telecommunications Policy Research Conference,* edited by G. Brock. Mahwah, N.J.: Lawrence Erlbaum Associates.

Economides, Nicholas, and Glen A. Woroch. 1992. "Benefits and Pitfalls of Network Interconnection." Discussion Paper EC-92-31, Stern School of Business, New York University.

Edell, Richard, Nich McKeown, and Pravin Varaiya. 1994. "Billing Users and Pricing for the TCP." Typescript, Department of Electrical Engineering and Computer Sciences, University of California, Berkeley.

Einhorn, Michael A. 1995. "Pricing and Competition Policies for the Internet." In *Public Access to the Internet,* edited by Brian Kahin and James H. Keller. Cambridge, Mass.: MIT Press.

Esbin, Barbara. 1998. "Internet over Cable: Defining the Future in Terms of the Past." Working Paper 30. Washington, D.C.: Federal Communications Commission, Office of Plans and Policy.

Farrell, Joseph, and Garth Saloner. 1985. "Standardization, Compatibility, and Innovation." *RAND Journal of Economics* 16 (1): 70–83.

Farrell, Joseph, and Garth Saloner. 1986. "Installed Base and Compatibility: Innovation, Product Preannouncements, and Predation." *American Economic Review* 76 (5): 940–55.

Federal Trade Commission. 1996. *Anticipating the 21st Century: Competition Policy in the New High-Tech, Global Marketplace.* Vol. 1, May.

———. 2000. *Privacy Online: Fair Information Practices in the Electronic Marketplace.* Federal Trade Commission Report to Congress. May.

Fishburn, Peter C., and Andrew Odlyzko. 1999. "Competitive Pricing of Information Goods: Subscription Pricing versus Pay-per-Use." *Economic Theory* 13 (2): 447–70.

Fishburn, Peter C., Andrew Odlyzko, and Ryan Siders. 1997. "Fixed Fee versus Unit Pricing for Information Goods: Competition, Equilibria, and Price Wars." In *Internet Publishing and Beyond: The Economics of Digital Information and Intellectual Property,* edited by Deborah Hurley, Brian Kahin, and Hal R. Varian. Cambridge, Mass.: MIT Press.

Forrester Research. 2000. "Internet Transaction Services." Forrester Report, April.

Galla, Preston. 1998. *How the Internet Works.* Indianapolis: Que.

Gandal, Neil. 1994. "Hedonic Price Indexes for Spreadsheets and an Empirical Test for Network Externalities." *RAND Journal of Economics* 25 (1): 160–70.

Gigante, Alexander. 1997. "'Domain-ia': The Growing Tension between the Domain Name System and Trademark Law." In *Coordinating the Internet,* edited by Brian Kahin and Janes H. Keller. Cambridge, Mass.: MIT Press.

Gillet, Sharon E., and Mitchell Kapor. 1997. "Self-Governing the Internet: Coordination by Design." In *Coordinating the Internet,* edited by Brian Kahin and James H. Keller. Cambridge, Mass.: MIT Press.

Goodman, Peter S. 2000. "AOL Ends Its Push for Open Access; Firm Had Lobbied to Share Cable Links." *Washington Post,* February 12.

Goolsbee, Austan. 1999. "Internet Commerce, Tax Sensitivity, and the Generation Gap." In *Tax Policy and the Economy,* edited by James Poterba. Vol. 14. Cambridge, Mass.: MIT Press.

———. 2000. "In a World without Borders: The Impact of Taxes on Internet Commerce." *Quarterly Journal of Economics* 115 (2): 561–76.

Goolsbee, Austan, and Peter Klenow. 1999. "Evidence on Learning and Network Externalities in the Diffusion of Home Computers." Working Paper 7329. Cambridge, Mass.: National Bureau of Economic Research.

Goolsbee, Austan, and Jonathan Zittrain. 1999. "Evaluating the Costs and Benefits of Taxing Internet Commerce." *National Tax Journal* 52 (3): 413–28.

Greenstein, Shane. 1999. "Framing Empirical Research on the Evolving Structure of Commercial Internet Markets." Paper presented at "Understanding the Digital Economy: Data, Tools and Research," Washington, D.C., May 25–26.

Groer, Annie. 2000. "Yard Sales Find a Home on the Internet." *Washington Post*, May 20.

Gupta, Alok, Dale O. Stahl, and Andrew B. Whinston. 1995. "A Priority Pricing Approach to Manage Multi-Service Class Networks in Real-Time." Paper presented at the MIT workshop on Internet economics, Cambridge, Mass., March 1995.

———. 1996. "An Economic Approach to Network Computing with Priority Classes." *Journal of Organizational Computing and Electronic Commerce* 6 (1): 71–95.

———. 1997a. "Economic Issues in Electronic Commerce." In *Readings in Electronic Commerce*, edited by Alok Gupta, D. O. Stahl, and Andrew B. Whinston. Reading, Mass.: Addison-Wesley.

———. 1997b. "Priority Pricing of Integrated Services Networks." In *Internet Economics*, edited by Lee W. McKnight and Joseph P. Bailey. Cambridge, Mass.: MIT Press.

———. 1997c. "Pricing of Services on the Internet." In *IMPACT: How IC² Research Affects Public Policy and Business Markets, a Volume in Honor of G. Kezmentsky*, edited by W. W. Cooper, G. E. Gibson Jr., Sten Thore, and F. Y. Phillips. Wesport, Conn.: Quorum Books.

Hagel, John III, and Arthur G. Armstrong. 1997. *Net Gain*. Harvard Business School Press.

Hagel, John III, and Marc Singer. 1999. *Net Worth*. Harvard Business School Press.

Hansel, Saul. 1999a. "Free-PC Will Be Acquired, Ending Computer Give-aways." *New York Times,* November 30.

———. 1999b. "IBM Plans to Pull Its PC's Out of Retail Outlets." *New York Times,* October 20.

Hartigan, Patti. 2000. "Music Industry Can't Outwit Online Outlaws." *Boston Globe,* May 31.

Herzog, Shai, Scott Shenker, and Deborah Estrin. 1997. "Sharing Multicast Costs." In *Internet Economics,* edited by Lee W. McKnight and Joseph P. Bailey. Cambridge, Mass.: MIT Press.

Huberman, Bernardo. 1997. "Storm Brewing on the Internet Horizon." Interview in *PC Week,* October 10.

International Competition Policy Advisory Committee (ICPAC). 2000. "Final Report to the Attorney General and Assistant Attorney General for Antitrust."

Internet Policy Institute. 1999. "Internet Policy Institute Launched as First Independent Think Tank on the Internet's Impact on Society." Press Release, November 9.

Jones, Jennifer. 2000. "Internet Tax Software Systems Being Readied." *Info World,* January 10.

Kaplan, Karen, and J. Shriver Jr. 1999. "U.S. May Soon End Its Reign of Domain Names." *Los Angeles Times,* September 29.

Katz, Michael L., and Carl Shapiro. 1985. "Network Externalities, Competition, and Compatibility." *American Economic Review* 75 (3): 424–40.

———. 1986. "Technology Adoption in the Presence of Network Externalities." *Journal of Political Economy* 94 (4): 822–41.

———. 1994. "Systems Competition and Network Effects." *Journal of Economic Perspectives* 8 (2): 93–115.

Kaufman, Leslie. 1999. "Selling Backpacks on the Web Is Much Harder Than It Looks." *New York Times,* May 24.

Kephart, Jeffrey O., and Amy Greenwald. 1998. "Shopbot Economics." Typescript, IBM Institute for Advanced Commerce.

Kopel, David B. 1999. "Access to the Internet: Regulation or Markets?" Heartland Policy Study 92, September 24.

Krol, E., and Klopfenstein, B. C. 1996. *The Whole Internet, Academic Edition: User's Guide and Catalog.* Sebastopol, Calif.: O'Reilly and Associates.

Kuttner, Robert. 1998. "The Net: A Market Too Perfect for Profits." *Business Week,* May 11, 20.

Labaton, Stephen. 2000. "White House and Agency Split on Internet Privacy." *New York Times,* May 23.

Lee, H. G. 1998. "Do Electronic Marketplaces Lower the Price of Goods?" *Communications of the ACM* 41 (1): 73–80.

Lehr, William, and Martin B. H. Weiss. 1996. "The Political Economy of Congestion Charges and Settlements in Packet Networks." In *The Internet and Telecommunication Policy: Selected Papers from the 1995 Telecommunications Policy Research Conference,* edited by G. W. Brock and G. L. Roston. Mahwah, N.J.: Lawrence Erlbaum Associates.

Lemley, Mark A. 1996. "Antitrust and the Internet Standardization Problem." *Connecticut Law Review* 28 (4): 1041–94.

Lewis, Tracy R., and David E. M. Sappington. 1994. "Supplying Information to Facilitate Price Discrimination." *International Economic Review* 35 (2): 309–27.

Liebowitz, S. J., and Stephen E. Margolis. 1994. "Network Externality: An Uncommon Tragedy." *Journal of Economic Perspectives* 8 (2): 133–50.

Litan, Robert E. 1999. "Balancing Costs and Benefits of New Privacy Mandates." Working Paper 99-3. AEI-Brookings Joint Center for Regulatory Studies.

Lukas, Aaron. 1999. *Tax Bytes: A Primer on the Taxation of Electronic Commerce.* Washington, D.C.: Cato Institute.

Macavinta, Courtney. 1999. "Simon and Schuster to Test Appeal of Online Books." *New York Times,* December 6.

Mace, Scott. 2000. "Enter Ipv6: New Protocol, Not a Root Canal or Forklift Upgrade." *Boardwatch,* February.

MacKie-Mason, Jeffrey K. 1999. "Investment in Cable Broadband Infrastructure: Open Access Is Not an Obstacle." Typescript, University of Michigan.

MacKie-Mason, Jeffrey K., and Varian, Hal R. 1993. "Some Economics of the Internet." Technical Report, University of Michigan.

———. 1995. "Pricing the Internet." In *Public Access to the Internet,* edited by Brian Kahin and James H. Keller. Cambridge, Mass.: MIT Press.

———. 1997. "Economic FAQs about the Internet." In *Internet Economics,* edited by Lee W. McKnight and Joseph P. Bailey. Cambridge, Mass.: MIT Press.

McKnight, Lee W., and Joseph P. Bailey, eds. 1997. *Internet Economics.* Cambridge, Mass.: MIT Press.

McLure, Charles E. Jr. 1998a. "Achieving a Level Playing Field for Electronic Commerce: Policy Considerations." *State Tax Notes,* June 1.

———. 1998b. "Electronic Commerce and the Tax Assignment Problem: Preserving State Sovereignty in a Digital World." Paper presented to the Institute of Professionals in Taxation/National Tax Association Joint Sales Tax Seminar, "Transactions Taxation: Telecommunications and Electronic Commerce," La Jolla, Calif., February 2–3.

———. 1999. "Electronic Commerce and the State Retail Sales Tax: A Challenge to American Federalism." *International Tax and Public Finance* 6 (2): 193–224.

Melamed, A. Douglas. 1999. "Network Industries and Antitrust." Address to the Federalist Society, Eighteenth Annual Symposium on Law and Public Policy, Competition Free Markets and the Law, Chicago, April 10.

Mendelson, Haim, and Johannes Ziegler. 1999. *Survival of the Smartest.* New York: John Wiley and Sons.

Mikesell, John L. 1970. "Central Cities and Sales Tax Rate Differentials: The Border City Problem." *National Tax Journal* 23 (2): 206–13.

Odlyzko, Andrew. 1996. "The Bumpy Road of Electronic Commerce." In *WebNet 96—World Conference, Web Society Proceedings,* edited by Hermann Maurer. AACE, 378–89.

———. 1997. "A Modest Proposal for Preventing Internet Congestion." Typescript, AT&T Labs–Research.

———. 1999a. "Paris Metro Pricing: The Minimalist Differentiated Services Solution." *Proceedings of the 1999 Seventh International Workshop on Quality of Service (IWQoS '99).* IEEE, 159–61.

———. 1999b. "Paris Metro Pricing for the Internet." *Proceedings of the ACM Conference on Electronic Commerce (EC-99).* ACM, 140–47.

Oppendahl, Carl. 1997. "Trademark Disputes in the Assignment of Domain Names." In *Coordinating the Internet,* edited by Brian Kahin and James H. Keller. Cambridge, Mass.: MIT Press.

Ordover, Janusz A., and Robert D. Willig. 1981. "An Economic Definition of Predation: Pricing and Product Innovation." *Yale Law Journal* 97 (November): 8–53.

———. 1999. "Access and Bundling in High-Technology Markets." In *Competition, Innovation and the Microsoft Monopoly: Antitrust in the Digital Marketplace,* edited by Jeffrey A. Eisenach and Thomas M. Lenard. Norwell, Mass.: Kluwer Academic.

Oxman, Jason. 1999. "The FCC and the Unregulation of the Internet." Working Paper 31. Washington, D.C.: Federal Communications Commission, Office of Plans and Policy.

Philips, Louis. 1983. *The Economics of Price Discrimination.* Cambridge University Press.

Richtel, Matt. 1999. "Music Industry Fails to Meet Target for Start of Online Sales." *New York Times,* November 22.

Rob, R. 1985. "Equilibrium Price Distributions." *Review of Economic Studies* 52 (3): 487–504.

Robert, Jacques, and Dale O. Stahl. 1993. "Informative Price Advertising in a Sequential Search Model." *Econometrica* 61 (3): 657–86.

Robinson, Constance K. 1999. "Network Effects in Telecommunications Mergers: MCI WorldCom Merger: Protecting the Future of the Internet." Address to the Practicing Law Institute, San Francisco, August 23.

Rohlfs, Jeffrey. 1974. "A Theory of Interdependent Demand for a Communications Service." *Bell Journal of Economics* 5 (1): 16–37.

Rowley, James. 2000. "FTC to Review Automakers' Plan for Online Purchasing." *USA Today,* March 23.

Saloner, Garth, and Andrea Shepard. 1995. "Adoption of Technologies with Network Effects: An Empirical Examination of the Adoption of Automated Teller Machines." *RAND Journal of Economics* 26 (3): 479–501.

Salop, S. 1977. "The Noisy Monopolist: Imperfect Information, Price Dispersion, and Price Discrimination." *Review of Economic Studies* 44 (3): 393–406.

———. 1979. "Monopolistic Competition with Outside Goods." *Bell Journal of Economics* 10 (1): 141–56.

———. 1986. "Practices That (Credibly) Facilitate Oligopoly Co-ordination." In *New Developments in the Analysis of Market Structure,* edited by Joseph Stiglitz and G. F. Mathewson. Cambridge, Mass.: MIT Press.

Salop, Steven, and Joseph Stiglitz. 1977. "Bargains and Ripoffs: A Model of Monopolistically Competitive Price Dispersion." *Review of Economic Studies* 44 (October): 493–510.

———. 1982. "A Theory of Sales: A Simple Model of Equilibrium Price Dispersion with Identical Agents." *American Economic Review* 72 (5): 1121–30.

Sarkar, Mitrabarun. 1997. "Internet Pricing: A Regulatory Imperative." In *Internet Economics,* edited by Lee W. McKnight and Joseph P. Bailey. Cambridge, Mass.: MIT Press.

Schmalensee, Richard. 1995. *Testimony on Antitrust Issues Related to Networks before the Federal Trade Commission.* Washington, D.C., December 1.

Schmitt, Eric. 2000. "AOL-Time Warner Pledge Questioned by Senate Panel." *New York Times,* March 1.

Schwartz, John. 2000a. "Intel Exec Calls for E-Commerce Tax." *Washington Post,* June 6.

———. 2000b. "Internet Tax Commission Ends Meeting in Deadlock." *Washington Post,* March 22.

Shapiro, Carl. 1999. "Exclusivity in Network Industries." *George Mason Law Review* 7 (3): 673–83.

Shapiro, Carl, and Hal R. Varian. 1997. "U.S. Government Information Policy." Paper presented at the Highlands Forum, Department of Defense, Washington, D.C., June 8.

———. 1999. *Information Rules: A Strategic Guide to the Network Economy.* Harvard Business School Press.

Shaw, Robert. 1997. "Internet Domain Names: Whose Domain Is This?" In *Coordinating the Internet,* edited by Brian Kahin and James H. Keller. Cambridge, Mass.: MIT Press.

Shenker, Scott. 1995. "Service Models and Pricing Policies." In *Public Access to the Internet,* edited by Brian Kahin and James H. Keller. Cambridge, Mass.: MIT Press.

Shenker, Scott, David D. Clark, and Lixia Zhang. 1993. "A Scheduling Service Model and a Scheduling Architecture for an Integrated Services Packet Network." Typescript.

Smith, Michael D., Joseph Bailey, and Erik Brynjolfsson. 1999. "Understanding Digital Markets: Review and Assessment." In *Understanding the Digital Economy,* edited by Erik Brynjolfsson and Brian Kahin. Cambridge, Mass.: MIT Press.

Srinagesh, Padmanabhan. 1997. "Internet Cost Structures and Interconnection Agreements." In *Internet Economics,* edited by Lee W. McKnight and Joseph P. Bailey. Cambridge, Mass.: MIT Press.

Stahl, Dale O. 1996. "Oligopolistic Pricing with Heterogeneous Consumer Search." *International Journal of Industrial Organization* 14 (2) : 243–68.

Stahl, Dale O., and Andrew B. Whinston. 1993. "An Economic Approach to Network Computing with Priority Classes." Working Paper. University of Texas at Austin, CISM.

Stiglitz, Joseph. 1987. "Competition and the Number of Firms in a Market: Duopolies More Competitive than Atomistic Markets?" *Journal of Political Economy* 95 (5): 1041–61.

Swindle, Orson. 1999. "Address to the Advisory Commission on Electronic Commerce." Williamsburg, Va., June 22.

Swire, Peter P., and Robert E. Litan. 1998. *None of Your Business: World Data Flows, Electronic Commerce, and the European Privacy Directive.* Brookings.

Swoboda, Frank, and Warren Brown. 1999. "Looking for a Net Profit." *Washington Post,* November 29.

Tapscott, Donald. 1996. *The Digital Economy: Promise and Peril in the Age of Networked Intelligence.* New York: McGraw-Hill.

———. 1998. *Growing up Digital: The Rise of the Net Generation.* New York: McGraw-Hill.

Thompson, Jim. 1999. "Web Caching—Savior or Fad?" *Boardwatch,* December.

———. 2000. "Caching Technology—Something for Everyone." *Boardwatch,* February.

Timberg, Craig. 2000. "Va. Assembly to Tackle the Future of Sales Tax." *Washington Post,* February 5.

Tirole, Jean. 1988. *The Theory of Industrial Organization.* Cambridge, Mass.: MIT Press.

Trandel, Gregory A. 1992. "Evading the Use Tax on Cross-Border Sales: Pricing and Welfare Effects." *Journal of Public Economics* 49 (3): 313–31.

Varian, Hal R. 1980. "A Model of Sales." *American Economic Review* 70 (4): 651–59.

———. 1989. "Price Discrimination." In *Handbook of Industrial Organization,* edited by R. Schmalensee and R. D. Willig. Vol. 1. New York: Elsevier Science B.V.

———. 1999a. "A Proposal to Eliminate Sales and Use Taxes." Typescript, University of California, Berkeley.

———. 1999b. "Buying, Sharing and Renting Information Goods." Typescript, University of California, Berkeley.

———. 1999c. "Estimating the Demand for Bandwidth." Typescript, University of California, Berkeley.

———. 1999d. "Market Structure in the Network Age." Typescript, University of California, Berkeley.

———. 2000. "Taxation of Electronic Commerce." Briefing to the President, Internet Policy Institute. April.

Vickrey, W. 1961. "Counterspeculation, Auctions, and Competitive Sealed Tenders." *Journal of Finance* 16 (1): 8–37.

Vita, Michael, and Frederick Horne. 1998. "Comment of the Staffs of the Bureaus of Economics and Competition of the Federal Trade Commission in the Matter of Improvement of Technical Management of Internet Names and Addresses." May 23.

Walsh, Michael J., and Jonathan D. Jones. 1998. "More Evidence on the 'Border Tax' Effect: The Case of West Virginia, 1979–1984." *National Tax Journal* 41 (2): 261–65.

Warren, Michael, and Michael White. 1999. "Web War Pits AT&T vs. AOL." *Washington Times,* July 28.

Washington State Department of Revenue. 1998. *Retailers' Cost of Collecting and Remitting Sales Tax.* Olympia.

Werbach, Kevin. 1997. "Digital Tornado: The Internet and Telecommunications Policy." Working Paper 29. Washington, D.C.: Federal Communications Commission, Office of Plans and Policy.

Wernerfelt, Birger. 1994. "On the Function of Sales Assistance." *Marketing Science* 13 (1): 68–82.

Wheeler, Julie. 2000. "Network Solution Sells Out." *Boardwatch,* May.

White, Lawrence J. 1999. *U.S. Public Policy toward Network Industries.* AEI-Brookings Joint Center for Regulatory Studies.

Winston, Clifford, and Chad Shirley. 1998. *Alternate Route: Toward Efficient Urban Transportation.* Brookings.

INDEX

Access, 1; equity issues, 32; government involvement, 32, 33–35, 82; growth trends, 29; historical development, 8; market dysfunction, 32–33; research needs, 107

Access pricing: accounting mechanisms, 31; auction approach, 18–21, 26; consumer demand, 31–32; dynamic priority pricing, 24–26; equilibrium user set, 70–71; equity issues, 32; expected capacity pricing, 28–29; flat pricing, 16–18, 26; government intervention, 33–34; limitations, 31–32; Paris Metro approach, 26–28; range of proposals, 15–16; rationale, 15, 30–31; research needs, 107; static priority pricing, 21–23, 26

Advanced Research Projects Administration (ARPA), 7

Advertising: brand recognition and loyalty, 61–62; search costs and pricing, 38–39

Advisory Commission on Electronic Commerce, 89–90, 91

Amazon.com, 3, 64

America Online, 18, 34, 81–82

Antitrust and monopoly issues, 4; abuse of market power, 84–86; business-to-business transactions, 109; collusion, 62–63, 66; digital transmission of entertainment products, 81; exclusivity provisions, 80–81; future of access, 33; industry compatibility, 73; infrastructure management, 77–79; innovation, 82–83; network effects, 77–78, 83, 85–86; predatory practice against new technology, 75; price discrimination in secondary markets, 64; product bundling strategies, 64–65; standards development, 79–80

ARPAnet, 7

Books.com, 53–54

Broadband services, 11; demand, 29; government regulation, 35;